How to Use Canon R6 Mark III EASILY

Beginner's Setup & Everyday Shooting Guide

Sammy Addy

Disclaimer

This book, *How to Use Canon R6 Mark III Easily: Beginner's Setup & Everyday Shooting Guide*, is an **independent educational guide** created to help users understand and operate the Canon EOS R6 Mark III camera.

This book is **not affiliated with, endorsed by, sponsored by, or approved by Canon Inc.** or any of its subsidiaries. Canon®, EOS®, and all related names, logos, and trademarks are the property of their respective owners and are used in this book **solely for identification and instructional purposes**.

The information provided in this book is based on practical use, research, and user experience. While every effort has been made to ensure accuracy and clarity, camera firmware updates, settings options, or operational behavior may change over time. The author and publisher **do not guarantee that all information will remain current or error-free**.

This book is intended for **educational purposes only**. The author and publisher shall not be held responsible for any damage to equipment, data loss, personal injury, or other issues resulting from the use or misuse of information contained in this book. Readers are encouraged to follow official safety instructions provided by the manufacturer and to use the camera responsibly.

By using this book, the reader acknowledges that **all camera operation decisions are made at their own discretion and risk**.

Chapter 1

Welcome to the Canon EOS R6 Mark III

What the Canon EOS R6 Mark III is (in simple terms)

The Canon EOS R6 Mark III is a full-frame mirrorless camera designed to shoot both photos and video at a high level. It's designed so you can shoot fast action, people, events, wildlife, and also record high-quality video without needing a cinema camera.

This book will not teach "general photography." Instead, it will teach you how to operate this specific camera—exactly where to press, where to find each menu item, what each setting does on the R6 Mark III, and when you should use it.

What you'll be able to do after using this guide

By the time you finish the book, you should be able to:

- Turn the camera on, set it up correctly, and format cards safely (inside the camera)
- Find your way around the camera's MENU tabs without confusion
- Change photo settings like ISO, drive mode, autofocus options, and image quality from the correct places
- Set up video recording options (resolution/frame rate), audio, and focus behavior for video
- Save your own preferred setup so the camera feels "personal" to you

Everything will be explained with real directions, like: "Press MENU → go to this tab → select this item → turn this dial → press SET."

How to Use Canon R6 Mark III Easily

The two places you control almost everything
On the R6 Mark III, you will change settings in two main ways:

1) Physical controls (buttons, dials, joystick, switches)
These are the things you press or turn directly on the body—like the shutter button, dials, the MENU button, the Q (Quick Control) button, and the joystick. The fastest changes usually happen here.

2) On-screen controls (the MENU and the Q screen)
When you need deeper settings (autofocus behavior, video recording formats, card setup, network features, customization), you'll use the MENU system. Canon also gives you a faster "control panel" called the Q screen, which lets you change common settings without digging deep.

We will cover both in a clean order, so you don't feel lost.

What "directional" means in this book
When you see a setting in this guide, it will always be explained like this:

- Where it is (the exact button or the exact menu path)
- How to access it (what to press and what to rotate)
- How to operate it (how to change it and confirm it)
- What it does (in plain language)
- When to use it (simple real-life examples)

So instead of "Use autofocus tracking for action," you'll get something like:
"Press MENU → go to the AF tab → select Subject to detect → choose People → then set Eye Detection to Enable."

This is a quick preparation checklist so the next chapters will be smooth:

Check 1: Have the basic items ready
- Camera body

How to Use Canon R6 Mark III Easily

- A charged battery (Canon recommends the LP-E6P for full performance on this model)
- A memory card (the R6 Mark III uses two card slots: one CFexpress Type B and one SD slot)
- A lens (RF or RF-S mount lenses attach to the camera's RF mount)

Check 2: Know where the official built-in manual is

Canon provides the R6 Mark III manual online at Canon's "cam. start" manual site. If you ever want Canon's official wording, you can cross-check there—but this book will explain everything in simpler language and clearer steps.

How this book is (so you never feel lost)

We will go in this order:

1. Physical tour of the camera (every button and port)
2. Basic setup (battery, cards, power, date/time, formatting)
3. Screen, viewfinder, and the Q screen
4. The MENU system (how to move through tabs and find settings)
5. Photos: focus, exposure, drive modes, image quality
6. Video: recording setup, frame rate/resolution, audio, focus for video
7. Customization, connectivity, troubleshooting, and practical "ready-to-shoot" setups

Chapter 2

Unboxing and Identifying Every Item

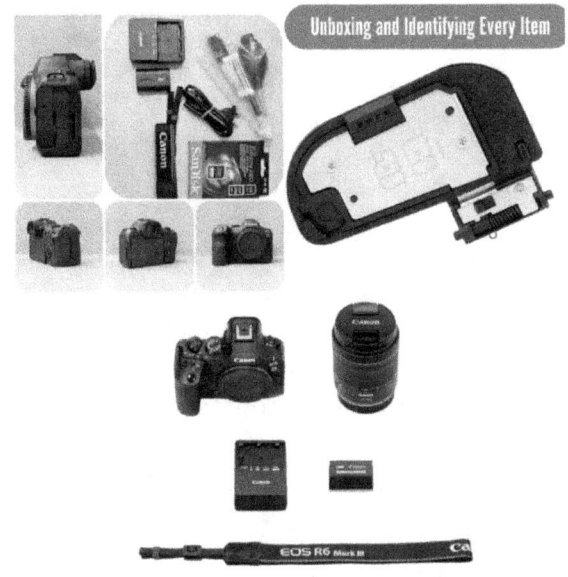

This chapter walks you through everything you should see when you open the Canon EOS R6 Mark III box, what each item is for, and where it fits on the camera. Do not rush this step. Correct handling at this stage prevents many beginner problems later.

Opening the box safely

Place the box on a flat surface like a table. Open the top flaps slowly. Inside, you will see cardboard compartments holding each item separately. Remove items one by one and place them on the table so you can identify them clearly.

Do not throw away the box or inner packaging yet. You may need them later for storage or transport.

Camera body (Canon EOS R6 Mark III)

This is the main camera unit.

When you pick it up:

- The large grip is on the right-hand side (this is where your fingers wrap around)

- The round opening at the front is the lens mount
- A plastic body cap is attached to protect the sensor

Do not remove the body cap yet. We will do that in the lens chapter.

Purpose of the camera body:

- This is where images and videos are captured
- All buttons, dials, menus, and ports are built into this unit

Battery

You will find one rechargeable battery in the box.

What it looks like:

- A small rectangular black battery with metal contacts on one side

Where it goes:

- Turn the camera upside down
- The battery compartment door is on the bottom of the camera, toward the grip
- Slide the door latch and open it
- The battery goes in with the metal contacts facing inward
- Push gently until it clicks into place

What it does:

- Powers the camera
- Without a charged battery, the camera will not turn on

Important beginner note:

- Always insert or remove the battery with the camera powered OFF

Battery charger

The charger may come as:

How to Use Canon R6 Mark III Easily

- A wall-plug charger with a removable battery slot, or
- A USB charging cable (depending on region)

How to use it:

- Insert the battery into the charger, matching the contact direction
- Plug the charger into a wall outlet or USB power source
- A light indicator shows charging status
- When charging is complete, remove the battery

When to use it:

- Charge the battery fully before first use
- A full charge ensures stable setup during initial configuration

Camera strap
The strap is a long fabric strap with two thin ends.

Where it attaches:

- Look at the left and right sides of the camera body
- You will see small metal strap loops on both sides

How to attach it:

- Thread the strap end through the metal loop
- Feed it back through the plastic buckle
- Pull tight so it cannot slip out
- Repeat on the other side

What it does:

- Prevents accidental drops
- Makes carrying the camera safer and more comfortable

Beginner tip:

- Attach the strap immediately before regular use

Body cap

The body cap is a round plastic cover attached to the front of the camera.

What it protects:

- The image sensor inside the camera

- Keeps dust and dirt out when no lens is attached

When to remove it:

- Only remove it when you are ready to attach a lens

- Never leave the camera open without a lens or cap

Hot shoe cover

This is a small plastic cover attached to the top of the camera.

Where it is:

- On top of the camera, above the viewfinder

What it protects:

- The hot shoe contacts (used for external flashes or accessories)

When to remove it:

- Only when attaching a flash or accessory

- Keep it safe so you can put it back later

Manuals and paperwork

Inside the box, you may also find:

- Quick start guide

- Warranty card

- Safety information leaflet

What to do with them:

- Keep them together in a safe place

- This book will explain things more clearly, but warranty papers are important

Items that may NOT be included

Depending on region, these items may not be in the box:

- Memory card
- USB-C cable
- HDMI cable
- Lens (if you bought the body-only version)

This is normal. You can still use the camera once you insert a charged battery, memory card, and lens.

Quick check before moving on

Before continuing to the next chapter, confirm the following:

- Battery is charged
- Battery is inserted correctly
- Body cap is still on
- Strap is attached (recommended)
- Memory card is available (we will insert it soon)

Chapter 3

Tour of the Camera Body (Physical Controls)

This chapter explains every button, dial, port, and switch you can physically touch on the Canon EOS R6 Mark III. We will move slowly and clearly, starting from the top of the camera and explaining each control exactly as you see it when holding the camera in your hands. This camera is made by Canon, and the control layout is specific to this model.

Top of the Camera

When you hold the camera normally, with your right hand on the grip and the lens facing forward, the "top" of the camera is the flat surface you see above the lens and viewfinder.

We will begin with the Mode Dial, because it controls how the camera behaves when you take a photo or record video.

Mode Dial: where it is and how to turn it

The Mode Dial is located on the top-right side of the camera. It is a round dial with letters and symbols printed around it. You can see it clearly when you look down at the camera from above.

To identify it correctly:

- It is the largest rotating dial on the top surface
- It has click-stops as you turn it
- Each click lands on a different shooting mode

How to turn the Mode Dial:

- Place your thumb and index finger on the dial
- Rotate it left or right

- You will feel a firm click as it moves from one mode to another
- Stop turning when the white indicator line points to the mode you want

You do not need to press any button to turn the Mode Dial. It rotates freely with firm resistance so it does not move accidentally.

What the Mode Dial does:

The Mode Dial tells the camera how much control it should give you over shooting settings like exposure, autofocus behavior, and video recording.

When you turn the Mode Dial:

- The camera immediately switches to the selected mode
- The screen updates to reflect the new mode
- Some menus and options may change depending on the selected mode

When to use the Mode Dial:

You use the Mode Dial whenever you want to change how the camera shoots. For example:

- Switching from automatic shooting to manual control
- Changing from photo shooting to video recording
- Moving to a custom preset you saved earlier

Important beginner note:

Always look at the top screen or rear screen after turning the Mode Dial. This confirms that the camera is now operating in the mode you intended. At this stage, you do not need to fully understand what each mode does yet. The important thing to understand now is:

- Where the Mode Dial is

- How to rotate it

- That changing it immediately changes how the camera behaves

Shutter Button: half-press vs full-press

The shutter button is one of the most important physical controls on the

Canon EOS R6 Mark III. It is the button you press to focus and take a photo.

Where the shutter button is located:

- The shutter button is on the top-right side of the camera

- It sits on the slanted part of the grip, exactly where your index finger naturally rests when holding the camera

- It is a round, slightly raised button

When holding the camera correctly:

- Your right hand grips the camera

- Your index finger rests lightly on the shutter button

- Your thumb stays behind the camera near the rear controls

The shutter button works in two stages. Understanding these two stages

is critical for getting sharp photos.

Half-press (first stage)

How to half-press the shutter button:

- Place your index finger on the shutter button

- Press down gently and slowly

- Stop pressing as soon as you feel a soft resistance or "click"

- Do not press all the way down

What happens during a half-press?

- The camera activates autofocus

How to Use Canon R6 Mark III Easily

- The camera measures exposure (brightness)
- Focus points appear on the screen or in the viewfinder
- The camera prepares itself to take the photo

How you know the half-press worked:

- You will see focus squares or boxes appear
- When focus is achieved, the focus box turns solid or changes color
- You may hear a small confirmation sound (if focus beep is enabled)
- The image in the viewfinder becomes sharp

What half-press is used for?

- Focusing on your subject
- Locking focus before taking a photo
- Checking that the camera can focus properly

Important beginner note:

If you press too quickly, you may skip the half-press stage. Always press slowly until you feel the first stop.

Full-press (second stage)

How to full-press the shutter button:

- Start with a half-press
- Once focus is confirmed, press the button all the way down
- You will feel a firmer click at the bottom

What happens during a full-press?

- The camera captures the photo instantly
- The image is saved to the memory card

How to Use Canon R6 Mark III Easily

- You may hear the shutter sound (unless silent mode is enabled)

What full-press is used for?

- Actually taking the photo
- Capturing the exact moment you want

Important beginner note:

If you full-press without waiting for focus confirmation, the photo may be blurry. This usually happens when the button is pressed too quickly.

Correct step-by-step way to take a sharp photo

1. Hold the camera steady with both hands
2. Place your index finger lightly on the shutter button
3. Half-press and wait for focus confirmation
4. Keep holding the half-press
5. Gently full-press to take the photo

This two-step action becomes natural with practice, but at first you must do it consciously.

Common beginner mistakes with the shutter button

- Pressing too hard and skipping the half-press
- Releasing the button too quickly after focusing
- Jerking the button instead of pressing smoothly
- Taking the finger off the button between focus and capture

Always think of the shutter button as having two levels, not one.

Main Dial: how to rotate it and what it controls

The Main Dial is a rotating control used to change important settings quickly while you are shooting. On the Canon EOS R6 Mark III, this dial works closely with the shutter button and is designed to be operated with your index finger.

Where the Main Dial is located:

- The Main Dial is on the top of the camera
- It sits directly behind the shutter button
- It is a textured, round wheel that rotates left and right
- You can feel the ridged edges with your finger

When holding the camera:

- Your right hand grips the camera
- Your index finger rests on or just behind the shutter button
- The Main Dial sits just behind that finger, easy to turn without changing grip

How to rotate the Main Dial:

- Use your index finger
- Roll the dial to the left or to the right
- You will feel clear clicking steps as it turns
- Each click changes a value on the screen

You do not press the Main Dial. It only rotates.

What the Main Dial controls (depending on mode):

The Main Dial changes different settings depending on which shooting mode the camera is currently in. The camera decides what the dial controls based on the Mode Dial setting.

In photo shooting modes:

How to Use Canon R6 Mark III Easily

- In Program (P) mode, rotating the Main Dial shifts the camera's chosen exposure combination
- In Shutter Priority (Tv) mode, rotating the Main Dial changes the shutter speed
- In Aperture Priority (Av) mode, rotating the Main Dial adjusts the aperture value
- In Manual (M) mode, the Main Dial usually changes shutter speed

You will always see the value change live on the screen or in the viewfinder as you rotate the dial.

In video mode:

- The Main Dial is commonly used to change shutter speed or exposure-related values for video
- The exact value being changed is shown on the screen as you rotate the dial

Inside the menu system:

- The Main Dial is used to scroll through menu options
- Rotating it moves the selection up or down
- Pressing the SET button (covered later) confirms your choice

How to know what the Main Dial is controlling at any moment:

- Look at the rear screen or electronic viewfinder
- The highlighted value is the one the Main Dial is changing
- If a number is flashing or highlighted, the dial is controlling that value

Step-by-step example (changing a value using the Main Dial):

How to Use Canon R6 Mark III Easily

1. Turn the Mode Dial to Av

2. Look at the screen and find the aperture value (for example f/4)

3. Rotate the Main Dial

4. Watch the number change as you turn the dial

5. Stop turning when the desired value appears

Important beginner notes:

- The Main Dial does nothing if the camera is turned off

- If nothing changes when you rotate it, the camera may be locked or in a mode where that value cannot be adjusted

- Always look at the screen to confirm what you are changing

The Main Dial is meant to be used while shooting, without taking your eye away from the viewfinder. With practice, you will adjust settings smoothly and confidently.

ISO Button: where it is and how to change ISO

The ISO button is used to control how sensitive the Canon EOS R6 Mark III's sensor is to light. On this camera, ISO is adjusted quickly using a dedicated button combined with a dial.

Where the ISO button is located:

- The ISO button is on the top of the camera

- It Is positioned near the shutter button and Main Dial

- It is a small, clearly labeled button marked "ISO"

- You can reach it easily with your right index finger without changing your grip

When holding the camera normally:

- Your right hand is on the grip

How to Use Canon R6 Mark III Easily

- Your index finger rests near the shutter button
- The ISO button sits close enough to press with that same finger

How to change ISO using the ISO button (step-by-step):

1. Turn the camera ON
2. Make sure the camera is in a photo or video shooting mode (not in playback or menu)
3. Press and hold the ISO button
4. While holding the ISO button, rotate the Main Dial
5. Watch the ISO value change on the screen or in the viewfinder
6. Release the ISO button when the desired ISO value is displayed

You do not need to press SET to confirm. The ISO change is applied immediately when you release the button.

How to know ISO is changing:

- The ISO number on the screen will increase or decrease as you turn the dial
- Example values you may see: ISO 100, ISO 400, ISO 1600, ISO 6400
- The selected value stays on screen briefly after you release the button

What ISO does on the Canon EOS R6 Mark III:

- Lower ISO values make images cleaner and less noisy
- Higher ISO values allow shooting in darker environments
- As ISO increases, image noise also increases

When to change ISO:

How to Use Canon R6 Mark III Easily

- Use lower ISO in bright light (outdoors, daylight)
- Increase ISO indoors, at night, or in dim environments
- Adjust ISO when the image looks too dark even after focusing

Using Auto ISO:

The camera can also control ISO automatically.

How to set Auto ISO:

1. Press and hold the ISO button
2. Rotate the Main Dial until "AUTO" appears
3. Release the ISO button

When Auto ISO is active:

- The camera automatically raises or lowers ISO based on lighting
- This is useful for beginners or fast-changing light conditions

Important beginner notes:

- ISO can only be changed when the camera allows exposure control
- In some fully automatic modes, ISO may be locked or controlled by the camera
- Always glance at the ISO value before shooting in low light to avoid unwanted noise

Common beginner mistakes:

- Forgetting ISO was set very high from a previous shoot
- Shooting in bright light with high ISO, causing unnecessary noise
- Pressing the ISO button but not turning the dial

If pressing the ISO button does nothing, check that:

How to Use Canon R6 Mark III Easily

- The camera is powered on
- You are not inside the MENU
- You are not in playback mode

Record (video) button: how to start and stop recording

The Record button is the control you use to start and stop video recording on the Canon EOS R6 Mark III. This button works independently from the shutter button and is dedicated specifically to video.

Where the Record button is located:

- The Record button is on the top of the camera
- It is positioned close to the shutter button
- It is smaller than the shutter button
- It is marked with a red dot or video symbol
- You can reach it easily with your right index finger or thumb, depending on your hand position

When holding the camera normally:

- Your right hand grips the camera
- Your index finger rests near the shutter button
- The Record button is slightly behind or beside the shutter button on the top plate

How to start video recording (step-by-step):

1. Turn the camera ON
2. Make sure a memory card is inserted
3. Set the Mode Dial to a mode that allows video recording
4. Point the camera at your subject
5. Press the Record button once

How to Use Canon R6 Mark III Easily

What happens when recording starts:

- A red recording indicator appears on the screen or in the viewfinder
- A timer begins counting the recording duration
- The camera starts capturing video and audio immediately
- Autofocus continues to operate during recording if enabled

You do not need to half-press the shutter button to record video. The Record button alone controls video capture.

How to stop video recording:

1. While recording is in progress, press the Record button again
2. The red indicator disappears
3. The timer stops
4. The video file is saved to the memory card

Always wait a moment after stopping recording to ensure the file finishes saving before turning the camera off.

How the Record button behaves in different situations:

- In photo shooting modes, pressing the Record button starts video recording instantly
- In video-focused modes, the Record button functions the same way
- You do not need to switch modes just to start recording basic video

How to confirm you are recording:

- Look for a red dot or "REC" indicator on the screen

- Check that the timer is counting upward
- If there is no red indicator, the camera is not recording

Important beginner notes:

- If you press the Record button and nothing happens, check that a memory card is inserted
- Recording cannot start if the card is full or not supported
- Some video settings may limit recording duration depending on resolution and frame rate

Common beginner mistakes:

- Forgetting to press the Record button again to stop recording
- Thinking the shutter button starts video recording
- Blocking the microphone with fingers while recording

Best practice:

- Always press the Record button deliberately
- Always confirm the red recording indicator before assuming video is being captured
- Stop recording before changing lenses or turning off the camera

Hot shoe: what it's for and what mounts here

The hot shoe is a mounting point on the Canon EOS R6 Mark III used to attach external accessories such as flashes and microphones. It also allows the camera to communicate electronically with those accessories.

Where the hot shoe is located:

- The hot shoe is on the top of the camera
- It sits directly above the electronic viewfinder
- It is a long, rectangular metal rail with electrical contacts inside

How to Use Canon R6 Mark III Easily

- When not in use, it is covered by a small plastic hot shoe cover

How to identify it correctly:

- Look at the top center of the camera
- You will see a straight slot running front to back
- The slot has metal edges and small contact points inside

What the hot shoe is used for:

- Mounting an external flash for brighter or controlled lighting
- Attaching a microphone for better audio during video recording
- Mounting other accessories designed to communicate with the camera

The hot shoe does not record anything by itself. It only acts as a connection point for accessories.

Removing the hot shoe cover:

1. Turn the camera OFF
2. Place your finger on the plastic hot shoe cover
3. Slide the cover straight backward (toward the rear of the camera)
4. Lift it off gently
5. Store it safely so it does not get lost

Always remove the cover before attaching any accessory.

Mounting an accessory on the hot shoe (step-by-step):

1. Turn the camera OFF
2. Align the accessory's mounting foot with the hot shoe slot
3. Slide the accessory forward into the slot until it stops
4. Tighten the locking wheel or lever on the accessory (if present)

5. Turn the camera ON

Once mounted correctly, the camera can communicate with the accessory through the hot shoe contacts.

What commonly mounts on the hot shoe:

External flash:

- Used to add light when shooting indoors, at night, or in low light
- The camera can control flash firing automatically
- Useful when the built-in lighting is not enough

Microphone:

- Used mainly for video recording
- Improves sound quality compared to the built-in microphone
- Ideal for interviews, talking-head videos, and events

Other accessories:

- Wireless transmitters
- LED light triggers
- Audio adapters designed for the hot shoe

What the hot shoe does NOT do:

- It does not hold the camera on a tripod
- It does not charge accessories unless they are designed to receive power
- It does not improve image quality unless an accessory is attached

Important beginner notes:

- Always turn the camera OFF before attaching or removing accessories

- Never force an accessory into the hot shoe
- Make sure accessories are fully seated and locked to prevent falling
- Do not touch the electrical contacts inside the hot shoe

Common beginner mistakes:

- Forgetting to remove the hot shoe cover
- Mounting accessories loosely
- Assuming the hot shoe records audio or light by itself

Best practice:

- Only attach accessories when needed
- Remove accessories when storing the camera
- Replace the hot shoe cover when no accessory is attached

Front of the Camera

Lens mount and lens release button

When you look at the Canon EOS R6 Mark III from the front, the most important parts you will see are the lens mount and the lens release button. These two parts work together to allow you to attach and remove lenses safely.

Where the lens mount is located:

- The lens mount is the large circular opening at the front of the camera
- It sits directly in the center of the camera body
- It is surrounded by a metal ring

- Inside the mount is the camera's image sensor (this is why it must be protected)

When the camera is new:

- A plastic body cap is attached to the lens mount
- This cap protects the sensor from dust and damage
- Do not touch anything inside the mount

What the lens mount does:

- It holds the lens firmly in place
- It allows the camera and lens to communicate electronically
- It ensures the lens aligns correctly with the sensor

The Canon EOS R6 Mark III uses the RF mount. Only lenses designed for this mount (or adapted correctly) should be attached.

Where the lens release button is located:

- The lens release button is on the front of the camera
- It is positioned to the right of the lens mount when you are facing the camera
- It is a small round button
- It is slightly recessed so it is not pressed accidentally

What the lens release button does:

- It unlocks the lens from the camera body
- It allows you to safely remove the lens
- It does nothing unless a lens is attached

How to attach a lens (step-by-step):

1. Turn the camera OFF

2. Place the camera on a stable surface or hold it securely

3. Remove the body cap from the camera by twisting it counterclockwise

4. Remove the rear cap from the lens

5. Look for the alignment mark on the lens

6. Look for the matching alignment mark on the camera mount

7. Line up the two marks

8. Insert the lens straight into the mount

9. Rotate the lens clockwise until you hear a click

Once you hear the click, the lens is locked and ready to use.

How to remove a lens (step-by-step):

1. Turn the camera OFF

2. Hold the camera firmly

3. Press and hold the lens release button

4. While holding the button, rotate the lens counterclockwise

5. When the lens stops turning, gently pull it away from the camera

6. Immediately place a cap on the lens and the body cap on the camera

Never release the lens without holding it. Always support it with your hand.

Important beginner notes:

- Always turn the camera OFF before changing lenses
- Never touch the glass inside the camera mount
- Avoid changing lenses in dusty or windy environments

- Always keep either a lens or body cap on the camera

Common beginner mistakes:

- Forgetting to press the lens release button before twisting
- Forcing the lens to rotate
- Leaving the camera open without a lens or cap
- Touching the sensor accidentally

Best practice:

- Change lenses with the camera facing downward to reduce dust entering
- Cap lenses immediately after removal
- Store unused lenses in a clean, dry place

Depth-of-field preview button (if present)

Depth-of-field preview button

On some Canon EOS R6 Mark III bodies, there may be a small button on the front of the camera that functions as a depth-of-field preview button. This button is optional depending on camera configuration and customization, so the first step is to confirm whether it is present and assigned on your camera.

Where to look for the button:

- Hold the camera facing you, with the lens pointing forward
- Look at the front of the camera body, near the lens mount
- Check the left side of the lens mount (from the photographer's point of view)
- The button is small, round, and slightly recessed

- It sits close enough to be pressed by your right-hand fingers while holding the camera

If you do not see a button in this position, or pressing it does nothing, it may be unassigned or set to a different function. Button customization will be explained later in this guide.

What the depth-of-field preview button does:

- It temporarily closes the lens aperture to the value you have set
- This lets you see how much of the scene will be in focus
- The preview happens before you take the photo
- The effect is visible in the viewfinder or on the rear screen

Normally, when you are not pressing this button:

- The lens stays wide open
- This keeps the viewfinder bright
- Depth of field is not shown accurately

When you press the depth-of-field preview button:

- The lens closes down to the selected aperture
- The image may appear darker
- You can see which parts of the scene are sharp and which are blurred

How to use the button (step-by-step):

1. Turn the camera ON
2. Set the Mode Dial to a photo shooting mode that allows aperture control
3. Point the camera at your subject

4. Look through the viewfinder or at the rear screen

5. Press and hold the depth-of-field preview button

6. Observe how the focus area changes in the image

7. Release the button to return to normal viewing

You must keep the button pressed to see the preview. Once you release it, the camera returns to its normal viewing state.

When to use the depth-of-field preview button:

- When you want to check background blur before taking a photo

- When shooting portraits and you want to confirm subject separation

- When photographing scenes where focus depth is important

Important beginner notes:

- The preview may look darker in low light

- This is normal and does not affect the final exposure

- The button does not take a photo

- It only previews focus depth

If the button does not work:

- The camera may be in a mode that does not support it

- The button may be reassigned to another function

- The camera may be in video mode

These situations will be addressed later when we cover button customization and shooting modes.

Best practice:

- Use this button when you want reassurance about focus depth

- Release it before taking the photo
- Do not hold it down while pressing the shutter button

Grip and how to hold the camera properly

The grip is the part of the Canon EOS R6 Mark III designed to help you hold the camera securely and comfortably. Holding the camera the right way is very important because it affects sharpness, stability, and how easily you can reach buttons and dials.

Where the grip is located:

- The grip is on the right-hand side of the camera when viewed from the back
- It is the thick, raised section with a textured rubber surface
- The shutter button, Main Dial, ISO button, and Record button are all positioned around this grip

The grip is shaped to fit your hand naturally, so your fingers fall into the correct positions without effort.

How to hold the camera with your right hand:

1. Wrap your right hand around the grip
2. Your fingers should curl naturally around the front of the grip
3. Your index finger rests lightly on the shutter button
4. Your middle finger supports the grip just below the shutter button
5. Your ring finger and little finger rest lower on the grip
6. Your thumb rests on the back of the camera near the rear buttons and joystick

How to Use Canon R6 Mark III Easily

Your right hand's main job is:

- Holding the camera securely
- Operating the shutter button
- Turning the Main Dial
- Pressing top buttons without shifting grip

How to support the camera with your left hand:

1. Place your left hand under the lens
2. Let the lens sit in your open palm
3. Use your left fingers to gently grip the lens barrel
4. Keep your left elbow close to your body for stability

Your left hand's main job is:

- Supporting the weight of the camera and lens
- Adjusting the lens zoom ring or focus ring
- Helping keep the camera steady

Never support the camera only with your right hand. The grip is designed for control, not full weight support.

How to hold the camera when shooting:

- Keep both hands on the camera
- Keep your elbows slightly tucked into your body
- Stand with your feet shoulder-width apart
- Breathe gently and avoid sudden movements when pressing the shutter button

This position reduces camera shake and makes your photos sharper.

How to hold the camera when using the viewfinder:

How to Use Canon R6 Mark III Easily

- Bring the camera up to your eye
- Press the viewfinder gently against your face
- This adds a third point of contact (hands + face)
- This improves stability, especially in low light

How to hold the camera when using the rear screen:

- Hold the camera slightly away from your face
- Keep both hands on the camera
- Avoid stretching your arms fully forward
- If possible, brace your elbows against your body

Common beginner mistakes:

- Holding the camera with one hand
- Letting the left hand hang free
- Gripping the camera too tightly
- Reaching for buttons instead of letting fingers rest naturally

What the grip is not for:

- It is not a carrying handle
- Do not lift the camera by the grip alone when a heavy lens is attached
- Always support the lens with your left hand

Best practice:

- Attach the camera strap and wear it around your neck or wrist
- Even when holding the camera correctly, the strap protects against drops

- Practice holding the camera correctly before shooting important moments

Once you are comfortable with the grip and hand position, using the buttons and dials becomes much easier and more natural

Back of the Camera

MENU button: exact location

The MENU button is the main entry point to all detailed settings on the Canon EOS R6 Mark III. Almost every advanced function—such as autofocus behavior, video settings, card setup, customization, and system options—is accessed through this button.

Where the MENU button is located:

- Turn the camera around so you are looking at the back
- Look at the upper-left area of the rear panel
- The MENU button is positioned to the left of the rear screen
- It is clearly labeled "MENU"
- It is a small, flat button designed to be pressed with your left thumb

You do not need to stretch your hand to reach it. It is placed so your left hand can operate it while your right hand stays on the grip.

How to press the MENU button:

- Hold the camera securely
- Use your left thumb
- Press the MENU button once firmly
- You do not need to hold it down

How to Use Canon R6 Mark III Easily

What happens when you press the MENU button:

- The camera switches from the shooting screen to the menu screen
- A set of tabs appears at the top of the screen
- Each tab contains a group of related settings
- The last-used menu page usually opens first

How to exit the menu:

- Press the MENU button again, or
- Half-press the shutter button

Either action returns you to the normal shooting screen.

When to use the MENU button:

- When you want to change camera settings that are not available on buttons or dials
- When setting up the camera for the first time
- When adjusting autofocus, video, playback, or system options
- When customizing buttons and controls

Important beginner notes:

- Pressing MENU does not take a photo or record video
- The MENU button works only when the camera is powered ON
- If the camera is busy saving a file, the menu may not open immediately

Common beginner mistakes:

- Pressing the Q button instead of MENU
- Expecting the MENU button to change settings by itself

- Forgetting to exit the menu before trying to shoot

Best practice:

- Use the MENU button for setup and configuration
- Use buttons and dials for quick shooting changes
- Always exit the menu before taking photos or recording video

INFO button: what it changes on screen

The INFO button controls what information is shown on the screen or in the viewfinder on the Canon EOS R6 Mark III. It does not change camera settings. Instead, it changes how much information you see while shooting or reviewing images.

Where the INFO button is located:

- Turn the camera to view the back
- Look near the top-right area of the rear panel
- The INFO button is labeled "INFO"
- It is positioned close to the rear screen
- It is designed to be pressed with your right thumb

The button is easy to reach without moving your hand off the grip.

What happens when you press the INFO button:

- Each press cycles through different display styles
- The shooting information on the screen changes
- The camera remains in the same shooting mode

You can press the INFO button repeatedly to move through all available display options.

How to Use Canon R6 Mark III Easily

What the INFO button changes during shooting:

When the camera is in shooting mode, pressing INFO cycles through views such as:

- A detailed shooting information display
- A cleaner screen with fewer icons
- A near-clear screen showing only essential information
- A screen optimized for framing the shot

The exact sequence depends on whether you are using:

- The rear screen, or
- The electronic viewfinder

How to use the INFO button (step-by-step):

1. Turn the camera ON
2. Make sure you are in photo or video shooting mode
3. Look at the rear screen
4. Press the INFO button once
5. Observe how the information layout changes
6. Press INFO again to cycle to the next display
7. Stop pressing when you see the display you prefer

What the INFO button changes during playback:

When viewing photos or videos:

- INFO cycles through different levels of image details
- You can see file information, shooting settings, or a clean image
- Each press adds or removes data from the screen

How to Use Canon R6 Mark III Easily

This is useful when reviewing images and checking details without entering the menu.

What the INFO button does not do:

- It does not change exposure, focus, or image quality
- It does not start or stop recording
- It does not open menus

Important beginner notes:

- The INFO button is safe to press anytime
- If the screen looks "too busy," press INFO to simplify it
- If information disappears, press INFO again to bring it back

Common beginner mistakes:

- Thinking INFO changes camera settings
- Forgetting that INFO works differently in shooting vs playback
- Pressing MENU when INFO is intended

Best practice:

- Use INFO to reduce clutter when composing a shot
- Use INFO to check details when reviewing images
- Choose a display style that helps you focus without distraction

Q (Quick Control) button: how it works

The Q button, also called the Quick Control button, gives you fast access to commonly used settings without opening the full MENU. It is one of the most important buttons on the back of the Canon EOS R6 Mark III because it lets you make quick changes while shooting.

Where the Q button is located:

- Turn the camera to look at the back

How to Use Canon R6 Mark III Easily

- The Q button is on the right side of the rear screen
- It is clearly labeled with the letter "Q"
- It sits within easy reach of your right thumb
- You can press it without removing your hand from the grip

What the Q button does:

- It opens the Quick Control screen
- This screen shows a grid of important camera settings
- You can change these settings quickly using dials, the joystick, or the touchscreen

The Q button does not take photos and does not record video. It only opens and closes the Quick Control screen.

How to open the Quick Control screen:

1. Turn the camera ON
2. Make sure you are in photo or video shooting mode
3. Press the Q button once

What you see when the Quick Control screen opens:

- The normal shooting view is replaced by a control panel
- Several boxes appear on the screen
- Each box represents a setting such as ISO, drive mode, autofocus area, white balance, image quality, and others
- One box is highlighted to show it is selected

How to move around the Quick Control screen:

You can move between settings in three ways:

Using the joystick:

How to Use Canon R6 Mark III Easily

- Push the joystick up, down, left, or right
- The highlight moves between boxes

Using the dials:

- Turn a dial to move or change values, depending on the setting

Using the touchscreen:

- Tap directly on the setting you want to change

How to change a setting using the Q screen:

1. Press the Q button
2. Move the highlight to the setting you want to change
3. Turn the Main Dial or Rear Dial to adjust the value
4. Watch the value change on screen
5. Press SET or half-press the shutter button to confirm and exit

Changes made on the Q screen take effect immediately.

How to exit the Quick Control screen:

- Press the Q button again, or
- Half-press the shutter button

Both actions return you to the normal shooting screen.

When to use the Q button:

- When you want to change settings quickly without opening the full MENU
- When you are shooting and need fast adjustments
- When learning the camera and want to see settings visually

What the Q button does not do:

- It does not replace the full MENU

- It does not show deep system or customization settings
- It does not save settings automatically as presets

Important beginner notes:

- The Q screen changes slightly depending on photo or video mode
- Some settings may be unavailable depending on the selected shooting mode
- If a setting is greyed out, it cannot be changed in the current mode

Common beginner mistakes:

- Pressing MENU instead of Q when trying to change quick settings
- Forgetting to confirm changes before exiting
- Expecting all camera settings to appear on the Q screen

Best practice:

- Use the Q button for fast, everyday changes
- Use the MENU button for deeper setup and customization
- Get used to the Q screen early, as it speeds up camera operation greatly

AF-ON button

The AF-ON button is used to activate autofocus without using the shutter button. On the Canon EOS R6 Mark III, this button allows you to separate focusing from taking the photo, giving you more control over when the camera focuses.

Where the AF-ON button is located:

- Look at the back of the camera
- The AF-ON button is on the upper-right area of the rear panel

How to Use Canon R6 Mark III Easily

- It is positioned above the rear dial and near the joystick
- It is clearly labeled "AF-ON"
- It is designed to be pressed with your right thumb

Your thumb should naturally rest close to this button when holding the camera properly.

What the AF-ON button does:

- It starts autofocus when pressed
- It tells the camera to focus without taking a photo
- It works independently of the shutter button

When you press AF-ON, the camera focuses. When you release it, focusing stops.

How to use the AF-ON button (step-by-step):

1. Turn the camera ON
2. Make sure you are in a photo or video shooting mode
3. Aim the camera at your subject
4. Press the AF-ON button with your right thumb
5. Watch the focus box appear and lock onto the subject
6. Release the AF-ON button when focus is achieved
7. Press the shutter button fully to take the photo

In this method, the shutter button only takes the photo and does not control focus.

What happens on the screen when AF-ON is pressed:

- Focus points or boxes appear
- The camera adjusts focus

How to Use Canon R6 Mark III Easily

- When focus is achieved, the focus indicator confirms it
- The image becomes sharp in the viewfinder or on the screen

When to use the AF-ON button:

- When photographing moving subjects
- When you want to lock focus and recompose
- When you do not want the camera to refocus every time you press the shutter
- When shooting multiple photos at the same focus distance

Why beginners may find AF-ON useful:

- It gives you more control over focus timing
- It prevents accidental refocusing
- It helps reduce missed focus when taking multiple shots

Important beginner notes:

- AF-ON does not take a photo
- If you press AF-ON and nothing happens, autofocus may be disabled or reassigned
- The camera must be set to autofocus mode for AF-ON to work

Common beginner mistakes:

- Pressing AF-ON and expecting a photo to be taken
- Forgetting to press AF-ON before pressing the shutter
- Confusing AF-ON with the shutter half-press

If AF-ON does not seem to work:

- Check that the camera is not in manual focus
- Check that autofocus is enabled

- Button assignment may have been changed (covered later in customization)

Best practice:

- Try AF-ON after you are comfortable with half-press focusing
- Practice pressing AF-ON to focus, then shutter to shoot
- Use whichever method feels more natural for you

Joystick / multi-controller

The joystick, also called the multi-controller, is a small movable control used to move focus points, navigate menus, and make quick selections on the Canon EOS R6 Mark III. It gives you precise control without taking your eye away from the viewfinder.

Where the joystick is located:

- Look at the back of the camera
- The joystick is on the right side of the rear panel
- It sits above the rear dial
- It is a small, textured nub that can be pushed in multiple directions
- It is positioned so your right thumb can reach it easily

When holding the camera correctly, your thumb naturally rests close to the joystick.

What the joystick does:

- Moves the autofocus point or focus area
- Navigates menu items
- Selects options on the Q (Quick Control) screen
- Confirms selections when pressed inward

How to Use Canon R6 Mark III Easily

The joystick works in five ways: up, down, left, right, and press (center push).

How to move focus points using the joystick:

1. Turn the camera ON
2. Make sure you are in a photo or video shooting mode
3. Look through the viewfinder or at the rear screen
4. Push the joystick in the direction you want the focus point to move
5. Watch the focus box move across the frame
6. Stop pushing when the focus point is where you want it

This allows you to place focus exactly on your subject without recomposing.

How to select a subject or focus area:

- Push the joystick to move the focus area
- Press the joystick inward to confirm or activate selection
- The camera responds immediately

How to use the joystick in the menu:

1. Press the MENU button
2. Use the joystick to move up and down through menu options
3. Push left or right to switch between tabs (if enabled)
4. Press the joystick inward to select an item
5. Use dials or joystick to adjust values
6. Press inward again to confirm

How to use the joystick on the Q screen:

How to Use Canon R6 Mark III Easily

1. Press the Q button
2. Use the joystick to move between setting boxes
3. Press inward to activate a setting
4. Rotate a dial to change the value
5. Half-press the shutter button to exit

What pressing the joystick does:

- Pressing inward works like the SET button
- It confirms selections
- It activates highlighted options

Important beginner notes:

- The joystick does not take photos
- It does not start video recording
- Small movements give precise control—do not push too hard

Common beginner mistakes:

- Forgetting the joystick can be pressed inward
- Trying to rotate the joystick (it does not rotate)
- Using the touchscreen when the joystick would be faster

If the joystick does not respond:

- The camera may be in a mode where movement is locked
- Touch control may be active instead
- Button behavior may have been customized

Best practice:

- Use the joystick for fast focus point changes
- Use it when shooting through the viewfinder

- Practice moving focus without looking at the joystick

Once you are comfortable with the joystick, controlling focus and navigating settings becomes much faster and more precise.

Playback button

The Playback button is used to view photos and videos that have already been recorded on the Canon EOS R6 Mark III. It does not affect shooting or recording. It is only for reviewing what is stored on the memory card.

Where the Playback button is located:

- Look at the back of the camera
- The Playback button is on the lower-right side of the rear panel
- It is positioned below the joystick and near the bottom corner
- It is marked with a triangle ▶ symbol
- It is designed to be pressed with your right thumb

You can reach this button easily without moving your hand off the grip.

What the Playback button does:

- It switches the camera from shooting mode to playback mode
- It displays the last photo or video you recorded
- It allows you to review, zoom, scroll, and inspect files

Pressing the Playback button does not open menus and does not change camera settings.

How to enter playback mode:

1. Turn the camera ON
2. Press the Playback button once
3. The most recent photo or video appears on the screen

How to Use Canon R6 Mark III Easily

The camera immediately stops showing the live shooting view and switches to stored content.

How to move between photos and videos:

- Turn the Main Dial or Rear Dial to scroll forward or backward
- Swipe left or right on the touchscreen
- Each movement displays a different file

How to view videos in playback:

1. Scroll to a video file (identified by a video icon)
2. Press the SET button or tap the play icon on the screen
3. The video starts playing
4. Press SET again to pause or stop

How to zoom in on a photo:

1. While viewing a photo, use the zoom control or touchscreen
2. Turn the dial or pinch on the screen to zoom in
3. Move around the image using the joystick or swipe
4. Zoom out to return to full view

This is useful for checking focus and sharpness.

How to exit playback mode:

- Press the Playback button again, or
- Half-press the shutter button

Either action returns the camera to shooting mode.

Important beginner notes:

- Playback mode does not drain the battery as quickly as recording, but extended reviewing still uses power

- If nothing appears, the memory card may be empty or not inserted
- Playback only shows files stored on the inserted card

Common beginner mistakes:

- Thinking playback means the camera is recording
- Forgetting to exit playback before trying to take a photo
- Assuming a photo is saved before seeing it in playback

Best practice:

- Quickly review important shots to confirm focus and exposure
- Avoid excessive playback during shooting to save battery
- Always exit playback before changing shooting settings

Delete button

The Delete button is used to remove photos or videos from the memory card inside the Canon EOS R6 Mark III. It only works during playback and does not affect shooting settings.

Where the Delete button is located:

- Look at the back of the camera
- The Delete button is on the lower-left side of the rear panel
- It is positioned below the MENU button area
- It is marked with a trash can icon
- It is designed to be pressed with your left thumb

What the Delete button does:

- It deletes the currently displayed photo or video
- It helps you remove unwanted files directly from the camera

- It only works when you are viewing images or videos in playback mode

The Delete button does nothing if the camera is in live shooting view.

How to delete a single photo or video (step-by-step):

1. Turn the camera ON
2. Press the Playback button to enter playback mode
3. Use the dial or swipe to display the photo or video you want to delete
4. Press the Delete button (trash can icon)
5. A confirmation message appears on the screen
6. Use the joystick or dials to select "Delete"
7. Press SET to confirm

Once confirmed, the file is permanently removed from the memory card.

How to cancel a delete action:

- When the confirmation screen appears
- Select "Cancel" instead of "Delete"
- Press SET
- The file remains untouched

What happens after deletion:

- The camera automatically shows the next available image
- The deleted file cannot be recovered through the camera
- Space on the memory card is freed

Important beginner notes:

- Deleting files cannot be undone

How to Use Canon R6 Mark III Easily

- Always confirm you are deleting the correct image
- Protected images cannot be deleted until protection is removed
- Deleting many files one by one can be slow

Common beginner mistakes:

- Pressing Delete while still in shooting mode and expecting something to happen
- Deleting a good image by rushing through confirmation
- Assuming deleting images improves camera performance

What the Delete button does not do:

- It does not format the memory card
- It does not delete all images at once
- It does not affect camera settings

Best practice:

- Delete obvious mistakes (completely blurred shots) during review
- Do bulk deletion by formatting the card when starting a new shoot
- Always back up important files before deleting

Rear dial and how it differs from the top dial

The Rear Dial is a rotating control on the back of the Canon EOS R6 Mark III. It works together with the top Main Dial, but it serves a different role. Understanding the difference between these two dials helps you change settings faster and with more control.

Where the Rear Dial is located:

- Look at the back of the camera
- The Rear Dial is on the right side of the rear panel

How to Use Canon R6 Mark III Easily

- It sits below the joystick and near the AF-ON button
- It is a circular wheel with textured edges
- It is operated with your right thumb

You can rotate the Rear Dial left or right. You do not press it to activate it.

What the Rear Dial does:

- It changes secondary settings
- It fine-tunes values while shooting
- It works alongside the top Main Dial

The camera decides what the Rear Dial controls based on the current mode and screen.

How the Rear Dial differs from the top Main Dial:

- The top Main Dial is operated with your index finger
- The Rear Dial is operated with your thumb
- The top dial usually controls the primary exposure value
- The rear dial usually controls the secondary exposure value

This separation allows you to change two settings without moving your hands.

How the Rear Dial works in common shooting modes:

In Aperture Priority (Av) mode:

- Top Main Dial changes the aperture
- Rear Dial adjusts exposure compensation

In Shutter Priority (Tv) mode:

- Top Main Dial changes the shutter speed
- Rear Dial adjusts exposure compensation

How to Use Canon R6 Mark III Easily

In Manual (M) mode:

- Top Main Dial controls shutter speed
- Rear Dial controls aperture

You will see the affected values change live on the screen or in the viewfinder as you rotate the dial.

How to use the Rear Dial step-by-step:

1. Turn the camera ON
2. Set the Mode Dial to a shooting mode
3. Look at the rear screen or viewfinder
4. Rotate the Rear Dial with your thumb
5. Watch the highlighted value change
6. Stop rotating when the desired value is set

How the Rear Dial works in menus:

- Rotating the Rear Dial scrolls through options
- It moves quickly through lists
- It helps change values without using the touchscreen

How the Rear Dial works in playback:

- It scrolls through images
- It helps review photos faster than button presses

Important beginner notes:

- The Rear Dial does nothing if the camera is turned off
- If a value does not change, it may be locked by the current mode
- Some dial functions can be customized later

Common beginner mistakes:

- Confusing the rear dial with the joystick
- Trying to press the dial instead of rotating it
- Expecting it to work the same way in every mode

Best practice:

- Think of the top dial as the main control
- Think of the rear dial as the fine adjustment control
- Practice using both together to build muscle memory

Once you understand both dials, adjusting settings becomes faster and smoother without needing to look away from your subject.

Sides and Bottom

Memory card slots and how to insert cards

The memory card slots are where the Canon EOS R6 Mark III stores photos and videos. This camera uses **two separate card slots**, allowing you to record to one card or both cards at the same time, depending on how you set it up later.

Where the memory card slots are located:

- Hold the camera normally
- Look at the **left side of the camera body** (from the photographer's point of view)
- You will see a rectangular door with a small latch
- This door covers the memory card slots

The card slots are not on the bottom. They are on the side so you can access them even when the camera is mounted on a tripod.

How to open the memory card door:

How to Use Canon R6 Mark III Easily

1. Turn the camera OFF

2. Place your thumb on the card door latch

3. Slide the latch in the direction indicated on the door

4. Gently swing the door open

Inside, you will see **two card slots stacked vertically**.

Understanding the two card slots:

- Slot 1: CFexpress Type B card slot

- Slot 2: SD card slot

Each slot is shaped differently so you cannot insert the wrong card type into the wrong slot.

Slot 1 (CFexpress Type B):

- This slot is usually at the top

- It accepts CFexpress Type B cards

- These cards are used for high-speed photo bursts and high-quality video recording

Slot 2 (SD card):

- This slot is usually below the CFexpress slot

- It accepts SD cards

- SD cards are commonly used for photos and standard video recording

How to identify which slot is which:

- Look closely next to each slot

- Small icons or labels indicate the card type

- The CFexpress slot is wider and thicker than the SD slot

How to Use Canon R6 Mark III Easily

How to insert a CFexpress Type B card (step-by-step):

1. Hold the CFexpress card so the label faces you

2. Align the card with the CFexpress slot

3. Gently slide the card straight into the slot

4. Push until you feel it seat firmly

5. Do not force it

The card goes in one direction only. If it does not slide in smoothly, stop and check orientation.

How to insert an SD card (step-by-step):

1. Hold the SD card with the label facing you

2. Align it with the SD slot

3. Slide it in gently

4. Push until it clicks into place

When properly inserted, the card will sit flush inside the slot.

How to remove a memory card:

1. Turn the camera OFF

2. Open the memory card door

3. Gently press the card inward

4. The card will pop out slightly

5. Pull it out carefully

Never pull a card out without pressing it first.

What happens when cards are inserted:

- The camera detects the cards automatically

- A card icon appears on the screen when the camera is turned on

- If the card is new or unformatted, the camera may prompt you to format it

Important beginner notes:

- Always turn the camera OFF before inserting or removing cards
- Never remove a card while the camera is writing data
- Look for the card access light and wait until it stops blinking
- For best performance, always format cards inside the camera

Common beginner mistakes:

- Forcing a card into the wrong slot
- Inserting cards upside down
- Removing a card while the camera is still saving files
- Using slow cards for high-quality video

Best practice:

- Decide which card slot you want to use as your main storage
- Use high-quality, reliable cards
- Keep spare cards in protective cases
- Format cards regularly inside the camera

Battery compartment

The battery compartment is where the Canon EOS R6 Mark III receives power. Without a properly inserted and charged battery, the camera will not turn on or function.

Where the battery compartment is located:

- Turn the camera upside down
- The battery compartment is on the bottom of the camera
- It is positioned directly beneath the hand grip

How to Use Canon R6 Mark III Easily

- You will see a rectangular door with a small latch

This placement keeps the battery secure and balanced during shooting.

How to open the battery compartment:

1. Turn the camera OFF
2. Hold the camera securely
3. Locate the battery compartment latch on the bottom
4. Slide the latch in the direction indicated by the arrow
5. The battery door will swing open

Do not force the door. It opens smoothly when the latch is fully released.

How to insert the battery (step-by-step):

1. Take the battery and look at the metal contact side
2. Inside the battery compartment, you will see matching metal contacts
3. Align the battery so the contacts match the direction shown inside the compartment
4. Slide the battery into the compartment
5. Push gently until you hear or feel a click

The click means the battery is locked in place.

How to close the battery compartment:

1. Gently swing the door back into position
2. Press until it closes firmly
3. Make sure the latch locks securely

The camera will not power on if the battery door is not fully closed.

How to remove the battery:

How to Use Canon R6 Mark III Easily

1. Turn the camera OFF

2. Open the battery compartment door

3. Inside, you will see a small battery release lever

4. Push this lever in the indicated direction

5. The battery will pop out slightly

6. Pull the battery out carefully

Always support the battery with your hand when removing it.

What happens when the battery is inserted:

- When you turn the camera ON, the screen activates

- A battery level icon appears on the screen

- The icon shows how much power remains

If the battery is low, the icon will change to warn you.

Important beginner notes:

- Always turn the camera OFF before inserting or removing the battery

- Never force the battery into the compartment

- Only insert the battery in the correct orientation

- Use fully charged batteries for setup and shooting

Common beginner mistakes:

- Inserting the battery backward

- Forgetting to fully close the battery door

- Removing the battery while the camera is still on

- Letting the battery drain completely before charging

Best practice:

How to Use Canon R6 Mark III Easily

- Charge the battery fully before use
- Carry a spare battery for longer shoots
- Remove the battery if storing the camera for a long time
- Keep battery contacts clean and dry

Once you are comfortable with the battery compartment, you are ready to power the camera reliably and safely.

USB-C port

The USB-C port on the Canon EOS R6 Mark III is used for charging, data transfer, and connecting the camera to other devices. This port allows the camera to communicate directly with computers, smartphones, and power sources.

Where the USB-C port is located:

- Hold the camera normally
- Look at the **left side of the camera body** (from the photographer's point of view)
- You will see a rubber or plastic port cover
- Lift or pull this cover gently to reveal the ports underneath
- The USB-C port is clearly labeled and has an oval-shaped opening

Do not force the port cover. It is designed to open easily.

What the USB-C port is used for:

- Charging the camera battery while it is inside the camera
- Transferring photos and videos to a computer or device
- Connecting the camera to a computer for file access
- Powering the camera from an external power source

How to connect a USB-C cable (step-by-step):

How to Use Canon R6 Mark III Easily

1. Turn the camera OFF
2. Open the side port cover
3. Take a USB-C cable
4. Insert the USB-C end gently into the USB-C port
5. Plug the other end into a power source or computer
6. Turn the camera ON if required

The cable should slide in smoothly. If it does not, do not force it.

Charging the camera using the USB-C port:

1. Insert a battery into the camera
2. Connect the USB-C cable to a compatible power source
3. The camera begins charging the battery
4. A charging indicator may appear on the screen or near the port

This is useful when traveling or when a wall charger is not available.

Transferring files to a computer:

1. Turn the camera OFF
2. Connect the USB-C cable to the camera and computer
3. Turn the camera ON
4. The computer detects the camera
5. Access photos and videos through the computer's file system

Always wait for file transfers to finish before disconnecting the cable.

Powering the camera via USB-C:

- The camera can operate while connected to a power source
- This is useful for long video recordings or studio setups
- Make sure the power source is stable and reliable

How to Use Canon R6 Mark III Easily

Important beginner notes:

- Do not remove the USB-C cable while files are transferring
- Always insert and remove cables gently
- Avoid bending or twisting the cable while connected
- Keep the port cover closed when not in use to protect against dust

Common beginner mistakes:

- Forcing the cable into the port
- Disconnecting during file transfer
- Using damaged or low-quality cables
- Leaving the port uncovered in dusty environments

Best practice:

- Use high-quality USB-C cables
- Turn the camera OFF before connecting or disconnecting when possible
- Close the port cover after use
- Use USB-C charging for convenience, not as a replacement for a fully charged spare battery

Sides and Bottom of the camera.

HDMI port

The HDMI port on the Canon EOS R6 Mark III is used to send live video and playback video from the camera to an external screen such as a TV, monitor, or recorder. This is especially useful for video recording, live monitoring, and reviewing footage on a larger display.

Where the HDMI port is located:

How to Use Canon R6 Mark III Easily

- Hold the camera normally
- Look at the left side of the camera body
- Open the same side port cover used for other connections
- Inside, you will find the HDMI port
- The HDMI port is smaller than a TV HDMI socket (micro HDMI type)

It has a flat, narrow shape and is clearly labeled.

What the HDMI port is used for:

- Displaying the camera's live view on an external monitor
- Viewing photos and videos on a TV or monitor
- Monitoring video while recording
- Sending video output to an external recorder

The HDMI port does not record video by itself. It only sends video from the camera to another device.

How to connect the camera to a TV or monitor (step-by-step):

1. Turn the camera OFF
2. Open the side port cover
3. Insert a micro HDMI cable into the HDMI port on the camera
4. Connect the other end of the cable to the HDMI input on the TV or monitor
5. Turn on the TV or monitor
6. Turn the camera ON

Once connected:

- The camera's screen content appears on the external display

How to Use Canon R6 Mark III Easily

- What you see on the camera screen is mirrored on the monitor

How to use HDMI during video recording:

1. Connect the HDMI cable as described above
2. Set the camera to a video-capable mode
3. Frame your shot using the external monitor
4. Press the Record button to start recording
5. The external screen shows exactly what the camera is capturing

This is helpful when:

- The camera is placed far from you
- You need a larger screen for accurate framing
- You want to avoid using the small rear screen

How to use HDMI for playback:

1. Press the Playback button on the camera
2. Photos and videos appear on the connected screen
3. Use the camera's dials or buttons to scroll through files
4. Videos play with sound through the connected device (if supported)

Important beginner notes:

- Always turn the camera OFF before connecting or disconnecting HDMI
- Use a proper micro HDMI cable made for cameras
- Do not pull the cable sharply while connected
- The HDMI port is delicate and should be handled carefully

Common beginner mistakes:

- Forcing a full-size HDMI cable into the port
- Disconnecting the cable while recording
- Expecting the HDMI port to power the camera
- Forgetting to select the correct HDMI input on the TV or monitor

Best practice:

- Use a short, flexible HDMI cable to reduce strain on the port
- Secure the cable if recording for long periods
- Close the port cover after disconnecting
- Avoid frequent plugging and unplugging unless necessary

Microphone and headphone jacks

The microphone and headphone jacks on the Canon EOS R6 Mark III are used for recording and monitoring audio during video recording. These ports are essential when you want better sound quality than the built-in microphone and when you need to hear exactly what the camera is recording.

Where the microphone and headphone jacks are located:

- Hold the camera normally
- Look at the left side of the camera body
- Open the side port cover (the same cover used for USB-C and HDMI)
- Inside, you will find two round audio ports
- Each port has a small icon next to it to indicate its function

One port is for a microphone, and the other is for headphones.

Identifying the microphone jack:

- The microphone jack is labeled with a microphone icon

How to Use Canon R6 Mark III Easily

- It is a 3.5mm round port
- This is where you plug in an external microphone

Identifying the headphone jack:

- The headphone jack is labeled with a headphone icon
- It is also a 3.5mm round port
- This is where you plug in headphones for audio monitoring

Do not confuse these two ports. Plugging accessories into the wrong jack will not work.

What the microphone jack is used for:

- Recording clearer and louder audio than the built-in microphone
- Capturing voices more accurately
- Reducing background noise when using directional microphones

How to connect a microphone (step-by-step):

1. Turn the camera OFF
2. Open the side port cover
3. Take your microphone's 3.5mm plug
4. Insert it gently into the microphone jack
5. Push until it fits snugly
6. Turn the camera ON
7. Set the camera to a video recording mode
8. Start recording using the Record button

Once connected, the camera automatically uses the external microphone instead of the built-in one.

What the headphone jack is used for:

How to Use Canon R6 Mark III Easily

- Listening to the audio being recorded
- Checking for noise, distortion, or low sound levels
- Monitoring audio in real time during recording

How to connect headphones (step-by-step):

1. Turn the camera OFF
2. Open the side port cover
3. Insert the headphone plug into the headphone jack
4. Push until it fits securely
5. Turn the camera ON
6. Enter video recording mode
7. Start recording or enable audio monitoring

You will hear the audio captured by the camera through the headphones.

How audio monitoring works:

- You hear sound as it is being recorded
- This helps you catch problems immediately
- If audio is too quiet, distorted, or missing, you will notice right away

Important beginner notes:

- These jacks are mainly active during video recording
- They do not affect photo shooting
- Always insert and remove audio plugs gently
- Do not pull cables sideways while connected

Common beginner mistakes:

- Plugging headphones into the microphone jack

- Forgetting to check audio levels before recording
- Assuming the camera records good audio automatically
- Leaving cables loose where they can be pulled out

Best practice:

- Always use an external microphone for important video recordings
- Wear headphones to monitor audio during recording
- Secure cables to avoid accidental disconnection
- Close the port cover when not using audio accessories

Once you understand how to use the microphone and headphone jacks, you gain full control over video sound quality.

Tripod mount

The tripod mount is the point where the Canon EOS R6 Mark III attaches to a tripod or other support systems. Using a tripod helps keep the camera steady and is important for sharp photos, long recordings, and precise framing.

Where the tripod mount is located:

- Turn the camera upside down
- Look at the bottom of the camera body
- The tripod mount is a round, metal threaded hole
- It is positioned near the center of the camera base, slightly toward the front
- It sits close to the battery compartment door

This threaded hole is designed to accept standard tripod screws.

What the tripod mount is used for:

How to Use Canon R6 Mark III Easily

- Attaching the camera to a tripod
- Mounting the camera on monopods, sliders, or other support systems
- Keeping the camera stable for long exposures
- Holding the camera steady for video recording
- Preventing camera shake when pressing buttons

The tripod mount does not power the camera and does not transfer data. It only provides physical support.

How to mount the camera on a tripod (step-by-step):

1. Turn the camera OFF
2. Set up the tripod on a stable surface
3. Locate the tripod's mounting screw on the tripod head
4. Align the screw with the tripod mount on the camera
5. Gently rotate the camera clockwise onto the screw
6. Tighten until the camera is secure
7. Do not over-tighten

Once mounted, lightly shake the tripod to confirm the camera is firmly attached.

How to remove the camera from a tripod:

1. Turn the camera OFF
2. Hold the camera securely with one hand
3. Loosen the tripod's mounting screw
4. Rotate the camera counterclockwise
5. Lift the camera away carefully

How to Use Canon R6 Mark III Easily

Always hold the camera before loosening the screw to prevent dropping it.

Important beginner notes:

- The tripod mount uses a standard thread size
- Do not force the camera onto a tripod screw
- Make sure the tripod is fully stable before letting go
- Be careful when opening the battery compartment while the camera is mounted, as access may be limited

Common beginner mistakes:

- Mounting the camera loosely
- Over-tightening the tripod screw
- Using unstable or lightweight tripods
- Forgetting to lock the tripod head

Best practice:

- Use a sturdy tripod appropriate for the camera and lens weight
- Always check that the tripod legs are locked
- Avoid touching the camera while recording video on a tripod
- Remove the camera carefully after use

With the tripod mount, you can achieve stable shots, smooth videos, and precise framing that are difficult to achieve when hand-holding the camera.

Chapter 4

Attaching and Removing a Lens

In this chapter, you will learn how to correctly attach and remove a lens from the Canon EOS R6 Mark III. This process is very important because the lens connects directly to the camera's sensor. Doing it the right way protects your camera, keeps images clean, and prevents damage.

We will go step by step, assuming you have never changed a lens before.

How to align the lens correctly

Before a lens can be mounted, it must be aligned properly with the camera's lens mount.

What to look for on the camera:

- On the front of the camera, around the circular lens mount, there is a small alignment mark
- This mark is usually a small colored dot or line
- It indicates where the lens should line up before mounting

What to look for on the lens:

- On the rear side of the lens, near the mounting ring, there is a matching alignment mark
- This mark is the same color and shape as the one on the camera
- It is designed to match exactly with the camera's mark

Why alignment matters:

- The lens will not attach correctly unless the marks arc aligned
- Forcing a misaligned lens can damage the mount
- Proper alignment ensures electronic contacts connect correctly

Before aligning:

- Make sure the camera is turned OFF
- Hold the camera securely
- Remove the body cap from the camera
- Remove the rear cap from the lens

Always keep the camera opening pointed slightly downward to reduce dust entering.

How to mount the lens step-by-step

Mounting the lens correctly ensures it locks securely and communicates properly with the camera.

Step-by-step process:

1. Turn the camera OFF
2. Hold the camera firmly with one hand
3. Hold the lens with the other hand
4. Locate the alignment mark on the camera
5. Locate the alignment mark on the lens
6. Line up the two marks carefully
7. Insert the lens straight into the camera mount
8. Once inserted, rotate the lens clockwise
9. Continue rotating until you hear or feel a click

The click means the lens is locked in place.

After mounting:

- Gently try to rotate the lens without pressing the release button
- If it does not move, it is properly locked

How to Use Canon R6 Mark III Easily

- Turn the camera ON
- The camera is now ready to shoot

If the lens does not click:

- Do not force it
- Remove the lens
- Realign the marks
- Try again slowly

How to remove the lens safely

Removing a lens must be done carefully to avoid dropping the lens or exposing the sensor unnecessarily.

Step-by-step process:

1. Turn the camera OFF
2. Hold the camera securely
3. Place one hand under the lens to support it
4. Locate the lens release button on the front of the camera
5. Press and hold the lens release button
6. While holding the button, rotate the lens counterclockwise
7. When the lens stops turning, gently pull it straight out
8. Immediately place the rear cap on the lens
9. Immediately place the body cap on the camera

Never let go of the lens while rotating it. Always support it with your hand.

Why turning the camera OFF matters:

- It reduces static charge that can attract dust
- It protects electronic contacts

- It prevents system errors

What the lens switches do (AF/MF, IS)

Many lenses designed for the Canon EOS R6 Mark III have small switches on the side of the lens barrel. These switches control how the lens behaves.

AF / MF switch:

- AF stands for Autofocus
- MF stands for Manual Focus

When the switch is set to AF:

- The camera controls focusing automatically
- Autofocus works using the shutter button or AF-ON button
- This is the default and recommended setting for beginners

When the switch is set to MF:

- Autofocus is disabled
- You must turn the lens focus ring by hand to focus
- The camera will not focus automatically

When to use AF:

- Everyday photography
- Moving subjects
- Portraits
- Video with autofocus enabled

When to use MF:

- Very low light situations
- Precise focus for still subjects

How to Use Canon R6 Mark III Easily

- When autofocus struggles

IS switch (Image Stabilization):

- IS stands for Image Stabilization
- This switch controls stabilization built into the lens

When IS is set to ON:

- The lens helps reduce camera shake
- Handheld shots appear steadier
- Video footage looks smoother

When IS is set to OFF:

- Stabilization is disabled
- Useful when the camera is mounted on a tripod
- Prevents unwanted movement correction

If your lens does not have an IS switch:

- Stabilization may be handled by the camera body instead
- This is normal

Always check the lens switches before shooting to make sure they are set correctly.

Beginner mistakes to avoid

These are common mistakes new users make when attaching or removing lenses. Avoiding them will protect your camera and lens.

Forcing the lens:

- Never force a lens to rotate
- If it does not turn smoothly, it is not aligned correctly

Changing lenses with the camera ON:

- Always turn the camera OFF

- This reduces dust and electronic issues

Touching the sensor:

- Never touch anything inside the camera mount
- The sensor is delicate and expensive to repair

Leaving the camera open:

- Always attach a lens or body cap immediately
- Do not leave the mount exposed

Dropping the lens:

- Always support the lens with one hand
- Especially important with larger or heavier lenses

Ignoring lens switches:

- Shooting in MF by accident can result in blurry images
- Leaving IS ON when mounted on a tripod can reduce sharpness

Best habits to develop:

- Change lenses in clean environments
- Keep caps accessible
- Work slowly and calmly
- Double-check alignment before twisting

Once you are comfortable attaching and removing lenses, the camera becomes much easier and safer to use.

Chapter 5

Powering On the Camera and First-Time Setup

This chapter guides you through turning on the Canon EOS R6 Mark III for the first time and completing the basic setup the camera requires before you start shooting. Every step is explained clearly, exactly as you will see it on the camera.

Power switch: where it is and how to turn the camera on

Where the power switch is located:

- Look at the top-right side of the camera
- The power switch is near the Mode Dial
- It is a small sliding switch with two positions: OFF and ON

How to turn the camera ON:

1. Make sure a charged battery is inserted
2. Slide the power switch from OFF to ON
3. The rear screen lights up
4. The camera becomes active

If nothing happens:

- Check that the battery is properly inserted
- Check that the battery door is fully closed
- Check that the battery has power

How to turn the camera OFF:

- Slide the same switch back to OFF
- Always turn the camera OFF when not in use

Turning the camera off helps save battery and protects the system.

First-time power-on screen

When you turn the Canon EOS R6 Mark III on for the first time, the camera automatically opens setup screens. These must be completed before normal use.

You will be guided through them one by one on the screen.

Language selection

What you will see:

- A list of available languages appears on the screen
- One language is highlighted

How to select a language:

1. Use the joystick or touch the screen
2. Move to your preferred language
3. Press SET to confirm

Once confirmed, all menus and messages will display in that language.

Date and time setup

After language selection, the camera asks for date and time.

Why this matters:

- Date and time are saved with every photo and video
- This helps with organization and sorting later

How to set the date and time:

1. Use the joystick to move between year, month, day, hour, and minute
2. Rotate a dial to change the value
3. Press SET to confirm each field
4. After setting all values, confirm to move forward

Set this carefully. Incorrect time stamps can cause confusion later.

Time zone selection
The camera may ask for your time zone.

How to set it:

1. Select your region from the list

2. Confirm with SET

This allows the camera to adjust time automatically when needed.

Inserting a memory card for the first time
Before the camera can save photos or videos, a memory card must be inserted.

What to do:

- Turn the camera OFF

- Open the memory card door on the left side

- Insert a compatible memory card into the correct slot

- Close the card door firmly

Turn the camera back ON.

If no card is inserted:

- The camera may show a warning

- You will not be able to record photos or videos

Formatting a memory card inside the camera
Formatting prepares the card to work properly with the Canon EOS R6 Mark III.

Why formatting is important:

- Ensures full compatibility

- Reduces file errors

- Clears old data safely

How to format the memory card (step-by-step):

1. Press the MENU button
2. Navigate to the setup menu (yellow tab)
3. Scroll to "Format card"
4. Select the card slot you want to format
5. Choose "OK"
6. Confirm formatting

The process takes only a few seconds.

Important notes about formatting:

- Formatting deletes all data on the card
- Always back up files before formatting
- Format new cards before first use
- Format cards regularly for best performance

Confirming the camera is ready

After completing first-time setup:

- The shooting screen appears
- No warning messages are displayed
- Battery and card icons appear on screen

This means the camera is ready for use.

Beginner checks before moving on

Before you journey on, confirm:

- Camera turns on and off normally
- Language is set correctly
- Date and time are correct

- Memory card is inserted and formatted
- No error messages appear

Once these basics are complete, you are ready to learn how to read and control what you see on the screen and viewfinder.

Chapter 6

Understanding the Screen and Viewfinder

LCD screen layout

The LCD screen on the Canon EOS R6 Mark III is the main screen on the back of the camera. It is where you see what the camera sees, check settings, review photos and videos, and interact with menus.

Where the LCD screen is located:

- Turn the camera to face the back
- The LCD screen covers most of the rear surface
- It is directly below the top buttons and to the right of the MENU button
- It is a color screen and also works as a touchscreen

The LCD screen turns on automatically when the camera is powered on, unless the viewfinder is being used.

What the LCD screen shows during shooting:

When the camera is in shooting mode, the LCD screen shows a live view of what the lens sees, plus shooting information layered on top.

The screen is divided into three main areas:

- The live image area (center)
- Shooting information (edges of the screen)
- Status icons (corners or sides)

Live image area:

- This is the main part of the screen
- It shows exactly what the camera is pointing at

- Any movement you see here will appear in your photo or video
- Focus boxes appear here when focusing

If something is not visible here, it will not appear in the final image.

Top area of the screen:

- Shows the current shooting mode
- Displays battery level icon
- Shows remaining shots or recording time
- Displays memory card status

These icons help you confirm the camera is ready before shooting.

Bottom area of the screen:

- Shows exposure-related information
- Displays values such as shutter speed, aperture, and ISO
- Shows exposure scale if applicable
- Indicates drive mode or recording status

These values change when you rotate dials or press buttons.

Focus and subject indicators:

- Focus points appear as small squares or boxes
- These boxes move when you use the joystick or touchscreen
- When focus is achieved, the box changes appearance
- This tells you the camera has locked focus

If focus boxes do not appear, autofocus may be disabled or set differently.

Status icons on the screen:

Depending on settings, you may see icons indicating:

- Autofocus mode

- White balance

- Image quality

- Stabilization status

- Audio levels (during video)

These icons give quick feedback without opening menus.

How the LCD screen responds to touch:

- You can tap to select focus points

- You can tap menu items

- You can swipe through photos in playback

- You can pinch to zoom in on images

Touch control can be enabled or disabled later in the menu.

How to change what appears on the LCD screen:

- Press the INFO button

- Each press cycles through different display layouts

- You can choose a detailed view or a cleaner view

This allows you to reduce clutter or see more information as needed.

Important beginner notes:

- The LCD screen does not change camera settings by itself

- It only displays information and allows interaction

- If the screen looks too busy, use the INFO button

- If the screen is blank, the viewfinder may be active instead

Common beginner mistakes:

- Ignoring warning icons on the screen

- Assuming the screen is broken when it is just set to a clean display
- Forgetting that touch input can move focus accidentally

Best practice:

- Always glance at the screen before shooting
- Confirm battery, card, and focus indicators
- Use a display layout that feels comfortable and clear

Touchscreen operations

The LCD screen on the Canon EOS R6 Mark III is a touchscreen. This means you can touch the screen directly to control certain camera functions instead of using buttons or dials. Touchscreen use is optional, but it can make the camera faster and easier to operate, especially for beginners.

What the touchscreen can be used for:

- Selecting a focus point
- Focusing on a subject
- Navigating menus
- Changing settings on the Q (Quick Control) screen
- Reviewing photos and videos
- Zooming in and out during playback

The touchscreen does not replace all buttons. Some actions still require physical controls.

How to use touch focus while shooting:

1. Turn the camera ON
2. Make sure the LCD screen is active

3. Point the camera at your subject

4. Tap directly on the subject on the screen

5. A focus box appears where you tapped

6. The camera focuses on that area

7. Press the shutter button to take the photo

This is useful when:

- You want to focus on a specific area quickly

- The subject is off-center

- You are shooting from an unusual angle

If tapping does nothing:

- Touch control may be disabled

- The camera may be using the viewfinder instead of the screen

How to take a photo using touch (if enabled):

Some setups allow the camera to focus and take a photo with one tap.

How it works:

- Tap the screen

- The camera focuses

- The shutter activates automatically

This feature can be enabled or disabled in the menu and is useful for quiet shooting or tripod work.

How to use the touchscreen in the menu:

1. Press the MENU button

2. Tap a menu tab at the top of the screen

3. Scroll by swiping up or down

4. Tap a menu item to open it

5. Tap options to change values

6. Tap "OK" or press SET to confirm

Touch input works the same way as a smartphone menu.

How to use touch on the Q (Quick Control) screen:

1. Press the Q button

2. Tap any setting box on the screen

3. A setting menu opens

4. Tap to select or adjust values

5. Exit by tapping outside or half-pressing the shutter button

This allows fast changes without using dials.

How to use touch during playback:

While reviewing photos or videos:

- Swipe left or right to move between images

- Pinch outward to zoom in

- Pinch inward to zoom out

- Drag to move around a zoomed image

- Tap play to start video playback

This makes image review fast and intuitive.

Important beginner notes:

- Touchscreen input only works when the LCD screen is active

- When using the viewfinder, touch input may be limited or disabled

- Accidental touches can move focus without you noticing

How to Use Canon R6 Mark III Easily

Common beginner mistakes:

- Touching the screen accidentally while holding the camera
- Moving the focus point without realizing it
- Thinking touch focus works in all modes automatically

Best practice:

- Use touch focus when shooting with the LCD screen
- Use buttons and joystick when shooting with the viewfinder
- Disable touch shutter if accidental photos occur
- Clean the screen regularly for accurate touch response

The touchscreen is a powerful convenience tool, but you stay in control of when and how it is used.

Viewfinder usage

The viewfinder on the Canon EOS R6 Mark III is an electronic viewfinder. It lets you look through the camera and see exactly what the camera is seeing, along with shooting information. Many users prefer the viewfinder because it is more stable and easier to see in bright light.

Where the viewfinder is located:

- Look at the back of the camera
- The viewfinder is centered at the top, above the LCD screen
- It is the small rectangular window you look through
- A soft rubber eyecup surrounds it to block stray light

How the viewfinder turns on:

- The camera automatically switches to the viewfinder when you bring your eye close to it
- There is a small eye sensor near the viewfinder

- When your eye moves away, the camera switches back to the LCD screen

You do not need to press any button to activate the viewfinder.

How to use the viewfinder (step-by-step):

1. Turn the camera ON
2. Hold the camera with both hands
3. Raise the camera to your eye
4. Look through the viewfinder
5. The LCD screen turns off
6. The viewfinder display turns on automatically

What you see in the viewfinder:

- A live view of what the lens sees
- Focus points or focus boxes
- Shooting information such as shutter speed, aperture, ISO, and battery level
- Recording indicators when shooting video

Everything you see in the viewfinder reflects the current camera settings in real time.

How to focus using the viewfinder:

- Half-press the shutter button, or
- Press the AF-ON button

Focus boxes appear inside the viewfinder. When focus is achieved, the box changes appearance to confirm focus.

Why many users prefer the viewfinder:

How to Use Canon R6 Mark III Easily

- It is easier to see in bright sunlight
- It provides better stability because the camera is pressed against your face
- It reduces camera shake
- It helps with precise framing and focus

Using the viewfinder adds a third point of contact (hands and face), which improves sharpness.

How to adjust the viewfinder for your eyesight:

Near the viewfinder, there is a small adjustment control.

How to adjust it:

1. Turn the camera ON
2. Look through the viewfinder
3. Rotate the small adjustment control beside the viewfinder
4. Stop when the information text looks sharp and clear

This adjustment does not affect photos. It only affects how the viewfinder looks to your eye.

How to change viewfinder display information:

- Press the INFO button while looking through the viewfinder
- Each press cycles through different display layouts
- You can choose more details or a cleaner view

How the viewfinder behaves during video:

- When recording video, the viewfinder shows the live video feed
- A red recording indicator appears
- Audio level indicators may appear if enabled

You can record video while using the viewfinder the same way you use the LCD screen.

Important beginner notes:

- The viewfinder does not take photos by itself
- If the viewfinder stays black, the LCD screen may be active instead
- If neither turns on, check battery power
- Smudges on the eyecup can reduce clarity

Common beginner mistakes:

- Forgetting the camera switches screens automatically
- Thinking the LCD is broken when the viewfinder is active
- Not adjusting the viewfinder for eyesight

Best practice:

- Use the viewfinder for steady shooting
- Use the LCD screen for low-angle or high-angle shots
- Adjust the viewfinder once and forget it
- Clean the eyecup occasionally

Switching between LCD and EVF

The Canon EOS R6 Mark III automatically switches between the LCD screen and the electronic viewfinder (EVF). Understanding how this switching works helps you avoid confusion when the screen suddenly turns off or changes.

How automatic switching works:

- The camera uses a small eye sensor near the viewfinder

- When the sensor detects your eye, the camera switches to the EVF
- When your eye moves away, the camera switches back to the LCD screen
- This happens instantly without pressing any button

This automatic behavior is the default setting and works during both photo and video shooting.

Where the eye sensor is located:

- Look just below or beside the viewfinder window
- You will see a small dark sensor area
- This sensor detects when your face is close to the viewfinder

Do not cover this sensor accidentally, or the screen may switch unexpectedly.

What happens when switching to the EVF:

- The rear LCD screen turns off
- The viewfinder display turns on
- All shooting information moves into the viewfinder
- Focus points, exposure values, and indicators remain visible

What happens when switching back to the LCD:

- The viewfinder turns off
- The rear screen turns back on
- You can use touch controls again
- The live view returns to the larger screen

How to manually control screen switching (if needed):

You can change how the camera switches between LCD and EVF through the menu.

Step-by-step:

1. Press the MENU button

2. Navigate to the setup menu (yellow tab)

3. Look for the screen or display settings

4. Select the option related to viewfinder or screen display

5. Choose how the camera switches screens

6. Confirm with SET

This allows you to:

- Force the camera to use only the LCD

- Force the camera to use only the EVF

- Use automatic switching (recommended for beginners)

When automatic switching is most useful:

- General photography

- Moving between eye-level and waist-level shooting

- Fast-paced shooting situations

When manual control may help:

- When the LCD keeps turning off unexpectedly

- When shooting video on a tripod

- When recording yourself and the screen switches unintentionally

Common beginner issues and fixes:

- Screen goes black suddenly: your hand or face may be near the eye sensor
- Touchscreen stops responding: EVF is active
- Viewfinder won't turn on: eye sensor may be blocked or disabled

Simple fixes:

- Move your hand away from the sensor
- Step back slightly from the viewfinder
- Check display settings in the menu

Best practice:

- Leave automatic switching enabled at first
- Learn to recognize when the EVF is active
- Switch manually only if automatic behavior becomes distracting
- Keep the eye sensor clean and uncovered

Understanding how the camera switches between the LCD and EVF helps you stay in control and prevents unnecessary frustration.

What the icons on the screen mean (camera-specific)

The Canon EOS R6 Mark III displays small icons on the LCD screen and in the electronic viewfinder to tell you the current status of the camera. These icons are **live indicators**. They change automatically based on how the camera is set and what it is doing.

Battery icon

Where you see it:

- Usually at the top of the screen
- Appears both on the LCD and in the EVF

What it shows:

- The remaining battery level

- Full icon means the battery is well charged

- Half icon means the battery is partially used

- Low icon means the battery needs charging soon

What to do:

- If the battery icon flashes or turns red, stop shooting and replace or recharge the battery

- Low battery can cause video recording to stop unexpectedly

Memory card icon

Where you see it:

- Near the top of the screen

- Often beside or near the battery icon

What it shows:

- That a memory card is inserted

- Which card slot is active

- Remaining shots or recording time

If the icon is missing:

- No memory card is inserted

- The card may not be recognized

If the icon flashes:

- The camera is writing data

- Do not remove the card or battery

Shooting mode indicator

Where you see it:

- Top or upper corner of the screen

How to Use Canon R6 Mark III Easily

What it shows:

- The current mode selected on the Mode Dial

- Examples include photo modes and video modes

Why it matters:

- Confirms how the camera will behave when you press the shutter or record button

- If the camera behaves differently than expected, always check this icon first

Shutter speed display

Where you see it:

- Bottom area of the screen

- Appears as a number like 1/250, 1/60, or similar

What it means:

- How long the camera captures light when taking a photo or video frame

- Faster numbers freeze motion

- Slower numbers allow more light

If the number blinks:

- The current setting may cause underexposure or overexposure

Aperture value display

Where you see it:

- Near the shutter speed value

- Appears as f/ followed by a number

What it means:

- Controls how much light passes through the lens

- Also affects background blur

If it does not change:

- The lens may not support adjustment
- The camera may be in a mode that locks aperture

ISO indicator

Where you see it:

- Bottom or side of the screen

What it means:

- Shows the current ISO sensitivity
- AUTO means the camera is controlling ISO
- Higher numbers indicate higher sensitivity

If ISO is very high:

- Image noise may increase
- This is normal in low light

Focus mode and focus box icons

Where you see them:

- Center of the screen
- Overlaid on the live image

What they show:

- Where the camera Is focusing
- The shape of the focus box
- Whether focus has been achieved

When focus Is successful:

- The focus box becomes solid or changes color

If focus keeps moving:

- Continuous autofocus may be active
- The camera is tracking a subject

Exposure level scale

Where you see it:

- Bottom center of the screen
- Looks like a horizontal line with marks and a pointer

What it means:

- Shows whether the image is too dark or too bright
- Centered pointer means balanced exposure
- Pointer to the left means darker
- Pointer to the right means brighter

This scale updates in real time as you change settings.

Image stabilization icon

Where you see it:

- On the shooting information area

What it shows:

- Whether stabilization is active
- Helps reduce camera shake

If the icon disappears:

- Stabilization may be turned off
- Or the camera is mounted on a tripod

Drive mode icon

Where you see it:

- Lower area of the screen

What it means:

- Shows how the camera takes photos
- Single shot, continuous shooting, self-timer, or silent mode

This icon helps you confirm whether the camera will take one photo or many when you press the shutter.

Video recording icons

When in video mode or recording:

- A red dot or REC indicator appears
- A timer shows recording duration
- Audio level meters may appear

If the red indicator is visible:

- The camera is actively recording video

If no red indicator:

- The camera is not recording, even if it looks like it is

Warning icons

You may occasionally see warning symbols such as:

- Overheating warning
- Card error
- Battery warning

These icons mean the camera needs attention before continuing.

Important beginner notes:

- Icons are not errors by default
- Most icons are informational
- Always glance at the top and bottom of the screen before shooting

- If something behaves unexpectedly, the screen icons usually explain why

Common beginner mistakes:

- Ignoring warning icons
- Shooting without checking card or battery status
- Confusing display icons with actual image problems

Best practice:

- Learn the meaning of the main icons gradually
- Do not panic when new icons appear
- Use the INFO button to simplify or expand the display
- Trust the screen as your camera's status dashboard

Chapter 7

Camera Modes Explained (Mode Dial)

Auto Mode

Auto Mode on the Canon EOS R6 Mark III is the camera's fully automatic shooting mode. In this mode, the camera makes almost all shooting decisions for you. This is designed for beginners who want to take photos without adjusting settings manually.

Where Auto Mode is on the Mode Dial:

- Look at the Mode Dial on the top-right of the camera
- Find the mode marked with the green AUTO icon
- This is the fully automatic mode

How to switch to Auto Mode:

1. Hold the camera securely
2. Rotate the Mode Dial until the green AUTO icon aligns with the white indicator line
3. Release the dial
4. The camera immediately switches to Auto Mode

You do not need to press any button to confirm.

What happens when Auto Mode is active:

- The camera controls shutter speed, aperture, and ISO automatically
- Autofocus is managed automatically
- The camera chooses focus points for you
- The camera decides whether flash or special features are needed

- Some menu options are limited to prevent confusion

The screen updates to show that Auto Mode is active.

What you can still control in Auto Mode:

Even though the camera controls most settings, you can still:

- Frame your shot
- Choose where to point the camera
- Decide when to press the shutter button
- Use the zoom ring on the lens
- Review photos using the Playback button

Touchscreen focus may also work, depending on how the camera is set.

What you cannot control in Auto Mode:

- You cannot manually set shutter speed
- You cannot manually set aperture
- You cannot manually set ISO
- Advanced menu options are restricted
- Some Q screen settings are locked

This is intentional. Auto Mode is meant to simplify operation.

How to take a photo in Auto Mode (step-by-step):

1. Turn the camera ON
2. Rotate the Mode Dial to Auto
3. Point the camera at your subject
4. Half-press the shutter button to focus
5. Wait for focus confirmation
6. Fully press the shutter button to take the photo

The camera decides the best settings based on the scene.

How the camera behaves in different scenes:

- In bright light, the camera uses lower ISO
- In low light, the camera raises ISO automatically
- If movement is detected, the camera adjusts settings to reduce blur
- If a face is detected, the camera prioritizes it for focus

All of this happens automatically without user input.

What you will see on the screen in Auto Mode:

- A simplified display
- Fewer icons and numbers
- Focus confirmation indicators
- Basic status icons like battery and card

This clean display helps beginners focus on composition instead of settings.

Using Auto Mode for video:

- Pressing the Record button starts video recording
- The camera automatically sets video exposure and focus
- Audio is recorded automatically
- Limited video settings are available

This is suitable for casual video recording.

Important beginner notes:

- Auto Mode is safe and reliable
- It is ideal for learning basic camera handling

- It prevents major setting mistakes
- If photos look different than expected, remember the camera is making decisions for you

Common beginner mistakes:

- Expecting manual control in Auto Mode
- Forgetting the camera may change settings between shots
- Assuming Auto Mode is the best choice for every situation

When to use Auto Mode:

- First-time use
- Family photos
- Travel snapshots
- Quick moments where there is no time to adjust settings

When to move beyond Auto Mode:

- When you want control over background blur
- When you want consistent exposure across shots
- When you want to learn how the camera works more deeply

Auto Mode is a starting point, not a limitation.

Program (P) Mode

Program Mode, shown as **P** on the Mode Dial, is the next step after Auto Mode on the Canon EOS R6 Mark III. In this mode, the camera still helps you by choosing exposure settings, but it also gives you direct control over important shooting options.

Where Program (P) Mode is on the Mode Dial:

- Look at the Mode Dial on the top-right of the camera
- Find the letter **P**

- Rotate the Mode Dial until **P** aligns with the white indicator line

The camera immediately switches to Program Mode.

What Program Mode does on the R6 Mark III:

- The camera automatically selects a matching shutter speed and aperture
- You gain access to many settings that are locked in Auto Mode
- You can override some camera decisions without going fully manual

This makes Program Mode ideal for beginners who want more control without complexity.

What changes when you switch from Auto to P Mode:

- The screen shows full shooting information
- You can change ISO
- You can use exposure compensation
- You can change autofocus settings
- You can use the Q (Quick Control) screen fully
- You can use Program Shift

The camera still protects you from extreme exposure mistakes.

How to take a photo in Program Mode (step-by-step):

1. Turn the camera ON
2. Rotate the Mode Dial to **P**
3. Point the camera at your subject
4. Half-press the shutter button to focus
5. Check the screen for focus confirmation

6. Fully press the shutter button to take the photo

The camera selects exposure automatically unless you adjust it.

What Program Shift is and how it works:

Program Shift allows you to change the camera's chosen shutter speed and aperture pair while keeping exposure balanced.

How to use Program Shift:

1. Set the Mode Dial to **P**
2. Half-press the shutter button to activate metering
3. Rotate the Main Dial
4. Watch the shutter speed and aperture values change together
5. Stop rotating when you like the combination

The camera keeps exposure balanced while shifting the values.

What Program Shift is useful for:

- Slightly freezing motion by choosing a faster shutter speed
- Slightly increasing background blur by adjusting aperture
- Making small creative adjustments without full manual control

Program Shift resets when:

- You turn the camera OFF
- You change the Mode Dial
- The camera enters sleep mode

What you can control in Program Mode:

- ISO (using the ISO button)
- Exposure compensation (using the Rear Dial)
- Drive mode

How to Use Canon R6 Mark III Easily

- Autofocus mode and area
- White balance
- Image quality
- Metering options

These controls are adjusted using buttons, dials, or the Q screen.

What you cannot control directly in Program Mode:

- You cannot independently lock shutter speed and aperture
- The camera still manages the exposure balance
- Full manual exposure requires Manual (M) mode

What you will see on the screen in P Mode:

- Shutter speed and aperture values
- ISO value
- Exposure scale
- Focus points
- Full status icons

This is a more informative display than Auto Mode.

Important beginner notes:

- Program Mode is not the same as Auto Mode
- The camera still helps, but you are more involved
- If photos look brighter or darker, check exposure compensation
- Program Shift does not harm the camera or image

Common beginner mistakes:

- Forgetting Program Shift resets automatically
- Thinking P Mode is fully manual

- Ignoring exposure compensation adjustments

When to use Program Mode:

- Everyday photography
- Learning how exposure values change
- Situations where lighting changes quickly
- When you want control without stress

Program Mode is often called a "learning mode" because it shows you how settings work.

Aperture Priority (Av)

Aperture Priority mode, shown as **Av** on the Mode Dial, lets you control the aperture while the Canon EOS R6 Mark III automatically selects the shutter speed needed for proper exposure. This mode is commonly used when you want control over background blur or how much of the scene stays in focus.

Where Aperture Priority (Av) is on the Mode Dial:

- Look at the Mode Dial on the top-right of the camera
- Find the letters **Av**
- Rotate the Mode Dial until **Av** aligns with the white indicator line
- Release the dial to lock the mode in place

The camera switches to Aperture Priority immediately.

What Aperture Priority does on the R6 Mark III:

- You choose the aperture value
- The camera automatically selects the shutter speed
- ISO can be set manually or left on Auto ISO
- Exposure updates live on the screen or in the viewfinder

The camera adjusts shutter speed every time lighting changes, but it keeps your chosen aperture constant.

How to change the aperture in Av mode (step-by-step):

1. Set the Mode Dial to **Av**
2. Look at the bottom of the screen or viewfinder
3. Find the aperture value shown as f/number (for example f/2.8 or f/8)
4. Rotate the **Main Dial** on the top of the camera
5. Watch the aperture number change as you rotate
6. Stop turning when the desired aperture value is displayed

The change takes effect immediately. No confirmation button is needed.

What aperture does on this camera:

- Smaller f-numbers (for example f/2.8) create more background blur
- Larger f-numbers (for example f/11) keep more of the scene in focus
- The selected aperture also affects how much light enters the camera

As you change the aperture, the camera automatically changes shutter speed to keep exposure balanced.

How the camera behaves after you change aperture:

- The shutter speed updates automatically
- If light is low, shutter speed may become slower
- If light is bright, shutter speed becomes faster

How to Use Canon R6 Mark III Easily

- You can see these changes live on screen

If the shutter speed becomes very slow, camera shake may occur. The camera will not warn you automatically.

Using exposure compensation in Av mode:

Exposure compensation allows you to tell the camera to make the image brighter or darker.

How to use it:

1. Stay in **Av** mode
2. Rotate the **Rear Dial**
3. Watch the exposure scale move left or right
4. Stop when the indicator is where you want it

This does not change your aperture. It only adjusts brightness.

What you can control in Av mode:

- Aperture (Main Dial)
- ISO (ISO button)
- Exposure compensation (Rear Dial)
- Autofocus settings
- Drive mode
- White balance
- Image quality
- Metering options

What the camera controls for you:

- Shutter speed
- Exposure balance (unless adjusted with compensation)

How to Use Canon R6 Mark III Easily

What you cannot control directly:

- Exact shutter speed selection
- Full exposure lock without using additional functions

What you will see on the screen in Av mode:

- Aperture value highlighted
- Shutter speed updating automatically
- ISO value displayed
- Exposure scale visible
- Focus points and status icons

This makes Av mode very informative and easy to monitor.

Common beginner mistakes in Av mode:

- Selecting a very small aperture and not noticing slow shutter speed
- Forgetting exposure compensation was adjusted earlier
- Expecting the camera to freeze motion automatically
- Ignoring shutter speed warnings (blinking values)

When to use Aperture Priority:

- Portraits (to control background blur)
- Landscape shots (to control depth of field)
- Everyday photography with creative control
- Situations where lighting changes but depth of field should stay consistent

When Av mode may not be ideal:

- Fast-moving subjects where shutter speed must be controlled

- Very low light without stabilization or tripod

Aperture Priority is one of the most useful modes on the Canon EOS R6 Mark III because it balances creative control with automatic safety.

Shutter Priority (Tv)

Shutter Priority mode, shown as **Tv** on the Mode Dial, lets you control the shutter speed while the Canon EOS R6 Mark III automatically selects the aperture needed for proper exposure. This mode is useful when you want direct control over motion—either freezing it or showing movement.

Where Shutter Priority (Tv) is on the Mode Dial:

- Look at the Mode Dial on the top-right of the camera
- Find the letters **Tv**
- Rotate the Mode Dial until **Tv** aligns with the white indicator line
- Release the dial to lock the mode

The camera switches to Shutter Priority immediately.

What Shutter Priority does on the R6 Mark III:

- You choose the shutter speed
- The camera automatically selects the aperture
- ISO can be set manually or left on Auto ISO
- Exposure updates live on the screen or in the viewfinder

The camera keeps your chosen shutter speed constant and adjusts the aperture as lighting changes.

How to change the shutter speed in Tv mode (step-by-step):

1. Set the Mode Dial to **Tv**
2. Look at the bottom of the screen or viewfinder
3. Find the shutter speed value (for example 1/500 or 1/60)

4. Rotate the **Main Dial** on the top of the camera

5. Watch the shutter speed value change as you rotate

6. Stop turning when the desired shutter speed is displayed

The change takes effect immediately.

What shutter speed does on this camera:

- Faster shutter speeds (for example 1/1000) freeze fast movement
- Slower shutter speeds (for example 1/30) allow motion blur
- Shutter speed also affects how much light reaches the sensor

As you change shutter speed, the camera automatically changes aperture to maintain exposure.

How the camera behaves after you change shutter speed:

- The aperture value updates automatically
- In bright light, the camera selects a smaller aperture
- In low light, the camera opens the aperture wider
- If the lens reaches its widest aperture and still cannot expose properly, the aperture value may blink

A blinking aperture value means the camera cannot achieve correct exposure with the current shutter speed.

Using exposure compensation in Tv mode:

Exposure compensation allows you to fine-tune brightness without changing shutter speed.

How to use it:

1. Stay in **Tv** mode

2. Rotate the **Rear Dial**

3. Watch the exposure scale move left or right

4. Stop when the indicator reaches the desired position

Your shutter speed remains fixed.

What you can control in Tv mode:

- Shutter speed (Main Dial)
- ISO (ISO button)
- Exposure compensation (Rear Dial)
- Autofocus settings
- Drive mode
- White balance
- Image quality
- Metering options

What the camera controls for you:

- Aperture
- Exposure balance (unless adjusted with compensation)

What you cannot control directly:

- Exact aperture selection
- Depth of field precision without changing shutter speed

What you will see on the screen in Tv mode:

- Shutter speed highlighted
- Aperture changing automatically
- ISO value displayed
- Exposure scale visible
- Focus points and status icons

How to Use Canon R6 Mark III Easily

This live feedback helps you understand how motion control affects exposure.

Common beginner mistakes in Tv mode:

- Choosing very fast shutter speeds in low light, causing underexposed images
- Ignoring blinking aperture warnings
- Forgetting exposure compensation adjustments
- Expecting background blur control in Tv mode

When to use Shutter Priority:

- Sports and action photography
- Wildlife and moving subjects
- Capturing fast moments without blur
- Intentional motion blur shots

When Tv mode may not be ideal:

- When background blur is the main goal
- When light is very low and aperture limits are reached

Shutter Priority gives you direct control over motion while the Canon EOS R6 Mark III handles exposure safely.

Manual (M)

Manual mode, shown as **M** on the Mode Dial, gives you full control over exposure on the Canon EOS R6 Mark III. In this mode, **you** decide the shutter speed and the aperture. The camera does not change these values for you. This mode is used when you want consistent results and complete control.

Where Manual (M) is on the Mode Dial:

- Look at the Mode Dial on the top-right of the camera
- Find the letter **M**
- Rotate the Mode Dial until **M** aligns with the white indicator line
- Release the dial

The camera switches to Manual mode immediately.

What Manual mode does on the R6 Mark III:

- You manually set shutter speed
- You manually set aperture
- ISO can be set manually or to Auto ISO
- The camera shows you exposure information but does not correct it for you

The camera will not stop you from underexposing or overexposing. It only **shows** you the result.

How to set shutter speed in Manual mode:

1. Make sure the Mode Dial is set to **M**
2. Look at the bottom of the screen or viewfinder
3. Locate the shutter speed value (for example 1/125)
4. Rotate the **Main Dial** on the top of the camera
5. Watch the shutter speed change as you rotate
6. Stop at your desired shutter speed

The shutter speed changes immediately.

How to set aperture in Manual mode:

1. Stay in **M** mode
2. Look at the aperture value shown as f/number

3. Rotate the **Rear Dial** with your thumb

4. Watch the aperture value change

5. Stop when the desired aperture is displayed

Shutter speed and aperture are now fully controlled by you.

How ISO works in Manual mode:

You have two choices for ISO.

Manual ISO:

- Press the ISO button

- Rotate the Main Dial

- Select a fixed ISO value

- You control all three exposure elements

Auto ISO in Manual mode:

- Press the ISO button

- Rotate the dial until **AUTO** appears

- The camera adjusts ISO automatically

- Shutter speed and aperture stay fixed

Auto ISO in Manual mode is useful when lighting changes but you want motion and depth of field to stay consistent.

Understanding the exposure scale in Manual mode:

- Look at the exposure level scale at the bottom of the screen

- A marker moves left or right as you change settings

- Centered marker means balanced exposure

- Marker left means darker image

- Marker right means brighter image

How to Use Canon R6 Mark III Easily

This scale is your guide. The camera does not correct exposure for you.

How to take a photo in Manual mode (step-by-step):

1. Set the Mode Dial to **M**
2. Set shutter speed using the Main Dial
3. Set aperture using the Rear Dial
4. Set ISO manually or to Auto
5. Check the exposure scale
6. Adjust settings until exposure looks right
7. Half-press the shutter to focus
8. Fully press the shutter to take the photo

What you can control in Manual mode:

- Shutter speed
- Aperture
- ISO
- Autofocus settings
- Drive mode
- White balance
- Image quality
- Metering behavior

What the camera still helps with:

- Autofocus
- Subject detection
- Image stabilization
- Exposure metering display

What the camera does not do in Manual mode:

- It does not adjust exposure automatically
- It does not prevent overexposure or underexposure
- It does not correct mistakes

What you will see on the screen in Manual mode:

- Shutter speed highlighted
- Aperture highlighted
- ISO value displayed
- Exposure scale clearly visible
- Focus points and status icons

This is the most information-rich display.

Common beginner mistakes in Manual mode:

- Forgetting to adjust ISO
- Ignoring the exposure scale
- Changing one setting and forgetting the others
- Shooting in changing light without Auto ISO
- Assuming Manual mode guarantees better photos

When to use Manual mode:

- Studio or controlled lighting
- Video recording with fixed exposure
- Scenes with consistent lighting
- Learning how exposure truly works
- Situations where the camera's automatic choices are not desired

When Manual mode may not be ideal:

- Fast-changing light
- Quick, unpredictable moments
- Beginners who are still learning exposure basics

Manual mode gives you full authority over the Canon EOS R6 Mark III. It rewards careful setup and consistency.

Scene Modes

Scene Modes are preset shooting modes designed to help the Canon EOS R6 Mark III recognize common shooting situations and apply suitable settings automatically. These modes are intended for beginners who want better results than Auto Mode without manually adjusting settings.

Availability note:

- Scene Modes may be grouped under a **Scene (SCN)** position on the Mode Dial or accessed through an on-screen scene selection
- Availability and exact presentation depend on how the camera is configured
- If your Mode Dial includes a Scene option, the following applies

Where Scene Modes are located:

- Look at the Mode Dial on the top-right of the camera
- Rotate the Mode Dial to the **Scene / SCN** position (if present)
- The camera switches to Scene Mode selection
- A list of scene types appears on the LCD screen

How to select a Scene Mode (step-by-step):

1. Turn the camera ON
2. Rotate the Mode Dial to **Scene / SCN**

3. Look at the LCD screen

4. Use the joystick, dials, or touchscreen to scroll through scene options

5. Highlight the desired scene

6. Press SET to confirm

Once selected, the camera adjusts settings automatically for that scene.

What Scene Modes do on the R6 Mark III:

- The camera chooses shutter speed, aperture, ISO, and autofocus behavior

- It prioritizes settings suitable for the selected scene

- Menu options are simplified to avoid confusion

- Focus behavior and color rendering may change automatically

You still control framing and when the photo is taken.

Common Scene Modes you may see and how they behave:

Portrait:

- Prioritizes subject separation

- Uses wider apertures when possible

- Focuses on faces automatically

- Background appears softer

Landscape:

- Prioritizes overall sharpness

- Uses smaller apertures

- Focuses across the scene

- Colors may appear more vivid

How to Use Canon R6 Mark III Easily

Close-up / Macro:

- Optimizes focus for close subjects
- Helps avoid focus hunting
- Suitable for flowers and small objects

Sports / Action:

- Uses faster shutter speeds
- Enables continuous autofocus
- Helps freeze moving subjects

Night / Low Light:

- Raises ISO automatically
- Uses slower shutter speeds if needed
- Helps capture more light
- May reduce camera shake effects

Food / Special scenes (if shown):

- Adjusts color and contrast
- Optimizes focus for close framing
- Enhances visual appeal automatically

What you can control in Scene Modes:

- Framing and composition
- Zooming the lens
- Basic drive modes
- Playback and review

What you cannot control in Scene Modes:

- Manual shutter speed selection

How to Use Canon R6 Mark III Easily

- Manual aperture selection
- Manual ISO selection
- Advanced autofocus customization
- Full Q screen access

The camera limits control intentionally to keep things simple.

What you will see on the screen in Scene Modes:

- The selected scene icon or name
- Simplified shooting information
- Focus confirmation indicators
- Basic battery and card status

This display is cleaner than P, Av, Tv, or M modes.

Common beginner mistakes with Scene Modes:

- Expecting full manual control
- Using the wrong scene for the situation
- Forgetting which scene is selected
- Assuming Scene Modes work well for every condition

When to use Scene Modes:

- When you are unsure which settings to use
- For quick results in common situations
- When handing the camera to someone else
- When learning how different scenes affect results

When to move beyond Scene Modes:

- When you want consistent results across shots
- When you want control over exposure or focus behavior

- When you are comfortable using P, Av, Tv, or M modes

Scene Modes are a helpful bridge between full Auto and manual control on the Canon EOS R6 Mark III.

Custom Modes (C1, C2, C3)

Custom Modes on the Canon EOS R6 Mark III allow you to **save complete camera setups** and recall them instantly by turning the Mode Dial. These modes are labeled **C1**, **C2**, and **C3** on the Mode Dial.

Each Custom Mode remembers how the camera was configured at the time you saved it, including exposure, focus behavior, drive mode, and many other settings.

Where Custom Modes are on the Mode Dial:

- Look at the Mode Dial on the top-right of the camera
- You will see **C1**, **C2**, and **C3**
- Rotate the Mode Dial until one of these aligns with the white indicator line
- The camera immediately switches to that saved setup

No confirmation button is required.

What Custom Modes do on the R6 Mark III:

- Recall a previously saved camera configuration
- Instantly change multiple settings at once
- Prevent you from having to reconfigure the camera repeatedly
- Provide consistent behavior for specific shooting situations

Each Custom Mode is independent. C1, C2, and C3 can all store different setups.

What settings are saved in a Custom Mode:

When you register a Custom Mode, the camera saves:

- Shooting mode (P, Av, Tv, or M)
- Shutter speed
- Aperture
- ISO or Auto ISO
- Autofocus mode and area
- Drive mode
- White balance
- Metering mode
- Image quality
- Many other shooting-related settings

When you switch to a Custom Mode, the camera recalls all of these instantly.

How to create and save a Custom Mode (step-by-step):

1. Turn the camera ON
2. Set the Mode Dial to the shooting mode you want to use (P, Av, Tv, or M)
3. Adjust the camera exactly how you want it
   - Set shutter speed, aperture, ISO
   - Set autofocus behavior
   - Set drive mode and other preferences
4. Press the MENU button
5. Navigate to the setup menu (yellow tab)

6. Find the option for registering custom shooting modes

7. Select "Register settings"

8. Choose **C1**, **C2**, or **C3**

9. Confirm with SET

The camera now stores that setup in the selected Custom Mode.

How to use a Custom Mode:

1. Turn the Mode Dial to **C1**, **C2**, or **C3**

2. The camera instantly switches to the saved configuration

3. Start shooting immediately

You do not need to reapply settings every time.

What happens if you change settings while using a Custom Mode:

- You can temporarily change settings while in a Custom Mode

- These changes apply only while the camera remains on

- When the camera is turned OFF and ON again, it returns to the saved Custom Mode settings

This prevents accidental permanent changes.

If you want to permanently update a Custom Mode:

- Make your changes

- Re-register the Custom Mode using the same steps as before

How to reset a Custom Mode:

- Re-register it with new settings

- Or overwrite it with a different configuration

There is no separate "reset" button for Custom Modes.

Practical examples of using Custom Modes:

- C1: Everyday photography setup
- C2: Action or sports setup
- C3: Video recording setup

These are only examples. You decide how each mode is used.

What you will see on the screen in Custom Modes:

- The mode indicator shows C1, C2, or C3
- Full shooting information is displayed
- All saved settings are active
- The camera behaves exactly as saved

This makes Custom Modes predictable and reliable.

Important beginner notes:

- Custom Modes do not update automatically
- If you forget to re-save, changes will be lost
- Custom Modes are based on your setup, not factory presets
- They are powerful but optional

Common beginner mistakes:

- Forgetting to register settings after adjusting
- Expecting Custom Modes to remember temporary changes
- Overwriting a Custom Mode accidentally
- Not knowing which setup is saved to which C mode

Best practice:

- Clearly decide what each Custom Mode is for
- Set it up carefully and test it
- Re-register if your shooting needs change

- Use Custom Modes for speed and consistency

Custom Modes turn the Canon EOS R6 Mark III into a camera that adapts instantly to your shooting style.

When and why to use each mode

This section explains **when to choose each Mode Dial option on the Canon EOS R6 Mark III** and **why that choice makes sense**, based strictly on how this camera behaves. Use this as a practical decision guide.

Auto Mode

When to use it:

- First time using the camera
- Quick snapshots where you don't want to think about settings
- Handing the camera to someone else to take a photo for you

Why to use it:

- The camera controls everything safely
- Prevents major exposure mistakes
- Simplified display reduces confusion
- Reliable results in common lighting

Why not to use it:

- You cannot control background blur or motion
- Many settings are locked
- Results may change from shot to shot without you knowing why

Program (P) Mode

When to use it:

- Everyday photography
- Walking around, travel, family moments

- Situations with changing light

Why to use it:

- The camera chooses safe exposure
- You can change ISO, autofocus, drive mode, and white balance
- Program Shift lets you fine-tune exposure behavior
- Full access to the Q screen and menus

Why not to use it:

- You do not fully control shutter speed or aperture independently
- Creative control is limited compared to Av, Tv, or M

Aperture Priority (Av)

When to use it:

- Portraits
- Landscapes
- Situations where background blur or depth of field matters
- Consistent-looking photos in changing light

Why to use it:

- You control aperture directly
- The camera handles shutter speed automatically
- Easy way to control how much of the scene is in focus
- Exposure adapts smoothly as light changes

Why not to use it:

- Shutter speed may become too slow in low light
- Not ideal for fast-moving subjects unless you monitor shutter speed

Shutter Priority (Tv)

How to Use Canon R6 Mark III Easily

When to use it:

- Sports and action
- Wildlife
- Children or pets moving quickly
- Intentional motion blur shots

Why to use it:

- You control motion directly
- The camera adjusts aperture automatically
- Easy way to freeze action or show movement
- Exposure adapts as lighting changes

Why not to use it:

- Depth of field control is limited
- In low light, the lens may hit aperture limits
- Blinking aperture warnings can occur

Manual (M) Mode

When to use it:

- Studio or controlled lighting
- Video recording with consistent exposure
- Scenes where lighting does not change
- Learning and mastering exposure
- Situations where auto exposure fails

Why to use it:

- Full control over shutter speed and aperture
- Consistent results across multiple shots
- No automatic exposure changes

- Works well with Auto ISO if needed

Why not to use it:

- Requires more attention
- Not ideal for fast-changing light
- Easy to underexpose or overexpose if not monitored

Scene Modes

When to use them:

- When you are unsure which settings to choose
- For quick results in specific situations
- Casual shooting without learning settings yet

Why to use them:

- The camera optimizes settings for the scene
- Reduces guesswork
- Cleaner display and simpler operation

Why not to use them:

- Very limited control
- Inconsistent results between scenes
- Not suitable for learning manual control

Custom Modes (C1, C2, C3)

When to use them:

- Repeated shooting situations
- Fast switching between photo and video setups
- Professional or semi-professional workflows

Why to use them:

- Instant recall of complex setups

- Consistent behavior every time

- Saves time and reduces mistakes

- Makes the camera feel personalized

Why not to use them:

- Requires setup and planning

- Changes must be re-registered to be permanent

- Can be confusing if you forget what is saved

Simple decision guide

- If you want the camera to decide everything → **Auto**

- If you want help but some control → **P**

- If you care about background blur → **Av**

- If you care about motion → **Tv**

- If you want full control and consistency → **M**

- If you want quick presets → **C1 / C2 / C3**

Understanding when and why to use each mode helps you choose the right tool instantly, instead of guessing.

Chapter 8

Practical Beginner Shooting Setups

Each setup is written so a beginner can **set the camera exactly as described**, without guessing. These are not theory lessons. They are **practical starting points** you can rely on and adjust later as you gain experience.

Everyday photography setup

This setup is for casual daily shooting such as family moments, street scenes, travel, and general use.

Mode and basic setup:

- Rotate the **Mode Dial** to **P (Program)**
- This allows the camera to handle exposure automatically

Autofocus:

- Press **MENU**
- Go to the **Purple Autofocus tab**
- Set **AF operation** to **One-Shot AF**
- Set **AF area** to **Whole area AF**
- Set **Subject to detect** to **People**
- Enable **Eye detection**

Image stabilization:

- Press **MENU**
- Go to **Image stabilization**
- Enable **In-body IS**
- If the lens has an IS switch, set it to **ON**

How to Use Canon R6 Mark III Easily

ISO:

- Press the **ISO button**
- Set ISO to **AUTO**

White balance:

- Press **MENU**
- Set **White Balance** to **Auto**

Picture Style:

- Select **Standard**

Why this works:

- The camera handles exposure
- Autofocus finds people automatically
- Stabilization reduces blur
- Minimal adjustments needed

This is the best "leave it on and shoot" setup.

Portrait setup

This setup is designed for photographing people with clear focus on the eyes and pleasing background blur.

Mode:

- Rotate the **Mode Dial** to **Av (Aperture Priority)**

Aperture:

- Turn the **Main Dial**
- Choose a **low f-number** (for example f/2.8 to f/4 if your lens allows)

Autofocus:

- Set **AF operation** to **One-Shot AF**
- Set **AF area** to **Whole area AF**

- Set **Subject to detect** to **People**
- Enable **Eye detection**

ISO:

- Set ISO to **AUTO**

Stabilization:

- Enable **In-body IS**
- Enable **Lens IS** if available

White balance:

- Set to **Auto**

Picture Style:

- Use **Standard** or **Portrait**

How to shoot:

- Position the subject in good light
- Half-press the shutter to confirm eye focus
- Press fully to take the shot

Why this works:

- The camera prioritizes eyes
- Background blur separates the subject
- Exposure adjusts automatically

Landscape setup

This setup is for scenery, buildings, nature, and wide scenes where detail across the frame matters.

Mode:

- Rotate the **Mode Dial** to **Av**

Aperture:

How to Use Canon R6 Mark III Easily

- Turn the **Main Dial**
- Choose **f/8 to f/11** for good depth of field

ISO:

- Set ISO to **100** or the lowest available value

Autofocus:

- Set **AF operation** to **One-Shot AF**
- Set **AF area** to **Whole area AF**
- Subject detection can be set to **None**

Stabilization:

- If handheld, keep **In-body IS ON**
- If using a tripod:
  - Turn **In-body IS OFF**
  - Turn **Lens IS OFF**

White balance:

- Set to **Auto** or **Daylight** for consistent color

How to shoot:

- Compose carefully
- Half-press to focus
- Use a tripod if possible for maximum sharpness

Why this works:

- Smaller aperture keeps the scene sharp
- Low ISO preserves detail
- Tripod use prevents blur

Video setup

How to Use Canon R6 Mark III Easily

This setup is for general video recording, including vlogging and simple content creation.

Mode:

- Rotate the **Mode Dial** to the **movie camera icon**

Resolution:

- Press **MENU**
- Set **Movie recording quality** to **Full HD 30p**

Autofocus:

- Enable **Movie Servo AF**
- Set **AF area** to **Whole area AF**
- Set **Subject to detect** to **People**
- Enable **Eye detection**

Stabilization:

- Enable **In-body IS**
- Enable **Lens IS** if available

Audio:

- Press **MENU**
- Set **Sound recording** to **Enable**
- Set recording level to **Auto** (or Manual if using an external mic)

White balance:

- Set to **Auto**

How to record:

- Press the **Record button**
- Watch focus box and audio meters

- Press Record again to stop

Why this works:

- Stable focus during recording
- Smooth handheld footage
- Clean audio with minimal setup

Low-light setup

This setup is for dim indoor scenes, night shots, or evening photography.

Mode:

- Rotate the **Mode Dial** to **Av**

Aperture:

- Choose the **widest aperture** your lens allows (lowest f-number)

ISO:

- Press **ISO**
- Set ISO to **AUTO**
- Allow the camera to raise ISO as needed

Autofocus:

- Set **AF operation** to **One-Shot AF**
- Set **AF area** to **Whole area AF**
- Use **People detection** if shooting people

Stabilization:

- Enable **In-body IS**
- Enable **Lens IS** if available

White balance:

- Set to **Auto**

How to shoot:

How to Use Canon R6 Mark III Easily

- Hold the camera steady
- Half-press to allow autofocus to lock
- Take the shot gently

Optional tripod use:

- Turn stabilization OFF
- Use a self-timer or remote shooting

Why this works:

- Wide aperture lets in more light
- Stabilization reduces hand shake
- Auto ISO adapts to changing light

Beginner best practice for all setups

- Start with these settings exactly
- Change only one thing at a time
- Review images after shooting
- Save your favorite setups to **C1, C2, or C3**
- Practice each setup in real situations

These practical setups turn the Canon EOS R6 Mark III into a **confident beginner camera that works with you**, not against you. Once these become familiar, you will naturally begin adjusting them to match your personal style.

Chapter 9

Final Tips for Confident Use

By this point, you already know where buttons are, how menus work, and how to set up the Canon EOS R6 Mark III correctly. What remains is learning how to **practice without stress, avoid frustration,** and **grow naturally** without feeling overwhelmed.

How to practice effectively

Effective practice is not about doing everything at once. It is about **repeating small actions until they feel natural**.

Start with one mode at a time

- Leave the camera in **P (Program)** for a few days
- Practice turning the camera on, focusing, and shooting
- Review images using playback
- Get comfortable holding the camera and pressing buttons

Practice menu navigation without pressure

- Turn the camera on at home
- Open the MENU and move through tabs slowly
- Do not change anything at first
- Just learn where things are

Practice with one subject

- Photograph the same subject multiple times
- Try it in daylight, shade, and indoor light
- Review focus and exposure after each session

Practice short sessions

How to Use Canon R6 Mark III Easily

- 15–20 minutes is enough
- Long sessions lead to fatigue and confusion
- Short sessions build muscle memory

Practice playback and review

- Zoom in to check focus
- Use INFO to view exposure
- Delete obvious mistakes
- Rate images you like

The goal of practice is **familiarity**, not perfection.

How to avoid common beginner frustration

Most frustration does not come from the camera. It comes from **expectations**.

Avoid changing many settings at once

- If something looks wrong, change one thing only
- Take another photo
- Compare results

Avoid comparing yourself to others

- Online photos are often edited
- Many were taken by experienced users
- Your goal is improvement, not competition

Avoid blaming the camera

- The R6 Mark III is very capable
- Most problems are setting-related
- Use Chapter 20 to troubleshoot calmly

How to Use Canon R6 Mark III Easily

Avoid learning everything in one week

- Cameras are tools, not exams
- Learning happens in layers
- Comfort comes before creativity

Avoid deleting everything immediately

- Keep early photos
- Compare them after a few weeks
- Seeing improvement builds confidence

Accept mistakes as part of learning

- Blurry photos are lessons
- Overexposed images teach exposure
- Missed focus teaches patience

Frustration fades when you slow down and stay curious.

Next steps to improve skills

Once you feel comfortable with basic operation, growth becomes enjoyable instead of stressful.

Save your favorite setups

- Use **C1, C2, and C3**
- Save setups that work for you
- This builds confidence and consistency

Practice intentionally

- One day for portraits
- One day for landscapes
- One day for video
- Focus on one goal per session

How to Use Canon R6 Mark III Easily

Review your images thoughtfully

- Ask simple questions:
    - Is it sharp?
    - Is it too bright or dark?
    - Is the subject clear?

Learn from your own photos first

- Your camera teaches you if you listen
- Patterns appear over time

Use remote shooting and apps

- Try remote shooting for stability
- Use image transfer to review on a bigger screen
- This helps you see details clearly

Gradually explore manual control

- Try Av mode more often
- Experiment with Manual only when comfortable
- There is no rush

Keep the camera accessible

- Store it where you can grab it easily
- Frequent use builds confidence faster than study

Final mindset for confident use

The Canon EOS R6 Mark III is not something you must "master" before enjoying. Confidence comes from:

- Knowing where things are
- Knowing how to fix problems
- Trusting yourself to experiment

How to Use Canon R6 Mark III Easily

You do not need to use every feature.

You do not need perfect photos.

You only need **consistent, calm practice**.

Each time you turn the camera on, you are improving—even if the photos are not perfect yet.

www.ingramcontent.com/pod-product-compliance
Lightning Source LLC
Chambersburg PA
CBHW060521290526
45791CB00001B/479